ROADS FROM
GETTYSBURG

by

John W. Schildt

BURD STREET PRESS

This Burd Street Press publication
was printed by
Beidel Printing House, Inc.
63 West Burd Street
Shippensburg, PA 17257-0152 USA

In respect for the scholarship contained herein, the acid-free paper used in this book meets the guidelines for permanence and durability of the Committee on Production Guidelines for Book Longevity of the Council on Library Resources.

For a complete list of available publications
please write
Burd Street Press
Division of White Mane Publishing Company, Inc.
P.O. Box 152
Shippensburg, PA 17257-0152 USA

Library of Congress Cataloging-in-Publication Data

Schildt, John W.
    Roads from Gettsburg / by John W. Schildt. -- 2nd
rev. ed.
        p.   cm.
    Includes bibliographical references (p.   ) and
index.
    ISBN 1-57249-071-3 (hardcover : alk. paper)
    1. Gettysburg (Pa.), Battle of, 1863.   I. Title.
E475.53.S38   1998
973.7'349--dc21   98-29223
                                                  CIP

PRINTED IN THE UNITED STATES OF AMERICA

To the memory of Major General John Buford, a key participant on the roads from Gettysburg

Contents

Illustrations

Maps

Introduction

The sun stood high in the sky, just a little past high noon. Its hot rays baked the fields of Pennsylvania, and the men of two armies faced each other on low ridges, approximately one mile apart. Beads of sweat stood on the foreheads of the soldiers; their blue and gray uniforms soaked with perspiration, giving a pungent smell to the uniforms. The men had been marching for several days and fighting for two. Flies buzzed as horses and mules pawed at the ground as though they knew something big was about to happen on this third day of July 1863 in the town of Gettysburg.

General Robert E. Lee had led his Army of Northern Virginia northward. If Lee could threaten Pennsylvania cities, and perhaps capture Harrisburg, the Confederate States of America might just become a free and independent nation. A victory north of the Potomac might bring economic and political recognition from European powers.

During the first two days of July, Lee had assaulted the flanks of the Army of the Potomac. Now, he was massing for an attack on the Union center. About 1 p.m. more than a hundred Confederate cannon commenced firing on the Union positions. The fields of Pennsylvania were quickly enveloped by white smoke. The din of exploding shells was deafening. Confederate soldiers wondered how anyone could withstand such a bombardment. One hour passed, then another. As Confederate batteries began to exhaust their ammunition, Major General James Longstreet nodded his head. It was a few minutes after three o'clock. All along Seminary Ridge, a long gray line rose up and moved out from the cover of the woods. They had a mile to go, across open fields to engage the foe. Twelve thousand five hundred men, part of "the flower of Lee's army," led by Generals George Pickett and Johnston Pettigrew, moved quickly across the fields.

From their positions on Cemetery Ridge, crouching behind stone walls and mounds of dirt, the soldiers of the Union II Corps watched and waited. The Confederates were advancing as though on parade. The columns were massed; the tattered battle flags fluttering in the breeze created by the rapid fire of the artillery. Occasionally portions of the attacking column virtually disappeared in the fog of the smoke. The Yankees felt profound admiration for their opponents.

As the men in gray and butternut reached the Emmitsburg Pike, the earth shook. Cannon and horses bolted in the air as the Union artillery and infantry responded with a storm of shot and shell. Confederate soldiers went down in heaps as some regiments, numbering fifty or less, almost disappeared. A few of the Confederates reached the "Bloody Angle" where there was hand-to-hand fighting. Then the attack, known today as Pickett's Charge melted away. In moments, large numbers of the Confederates were streaming back to the cover of Seminary Ridge. Five thousand were killed, wounded or missing in action. Those who survived were in a state of shock.

As the survivors reached Seminary Ridge, they were met by Robert E. Lee, near the location of the present Virginia State Monument. "It's all my fault," he said, "It's all my fault."[1]

1863.

	Sunday.	Monday.	Tuesday.	Wednesday.	Thursday.	Friday.	Saturday.
July...	....	....	....	1	2	3	4
	5	6	7	8	9	10	11
	12	13	14	15	16	17	18
	19	20	21	22	23	24	25
	26	27	28	29	30	31	....
Aug...	....	....	....	....	....	....	1

July 1863

The sun went down. The shades of night fell on the fields of Pennsylvania. The nation had never witnessed such a charge. Troops, physically, mentally, and emotionally exhausted, tried to rest. However, there was no rest in the medical corps of the armies. They worked throughout the night and for the next several days, with little or no rest. During the night, the medical people and soldiers wandered on both sides of the Emmitsburg Pike seeking to find and assist the wounded.

While the doctors treated the wounded, Robert E. Lee walked around his headquarters along the Chambersburg Pike, and pondered his situation. He had risked so much and come so close. But now that the attack on the Union center had failed, he had no alternative—but to retreat.

In a sense, the roads from Gettysburg began with the repulse of Pickett's Charge. Immediately afterward, Jed Hotchkiss, the erstwhile mapmaker of the Army of Northern Virginia noted "there was a general feeling of despondency."[2] Shortly after the repulse, there had been a council of war at Major General A. P. Hill's headquarters. "There was a general movement of wagons, wounded, and prisoners to the rear, and the unmistakable signs of a retreat were plentiful. They were headed for the Black Horse Tavern on the Fairfield Road.

—1—
"The Glorious Fourth"

Shortly after midnight, in the first moments of July 4, General Robert E. Lee sent for Brigadier General John Imboden. Lee was tired and had to make a decision. For three days he had dented the Union line, but was unable to break through it. Some of his lieutenants had not done their best, but he bore them no malice. Although not at his best physically, he mounted Traveler and rode in the moonlight. Some have called the midnight ride, "Lee's Gethsemane." So close, yet so far. He must return to Virginia. The longer he remained at Gettysburg, the more perilous the situation would become as he ran the risk of losing his lines of supply, communication, and retreat. While Lee would get weaker, Meade would become stronger.

During Lee's ride, John Imboden arrived at Lee's tent. Stretched out on the grass, Imboden waited almost an hour for his commander to return. Lee seemed too tired to dismount. Imboden rushed to assist the chieftain, but Lee leaned against Traveler and looked at the ground. The moon shone on the general's face revealing a sadness Imboden had never seen before. Imboden waited for General Lee to speak.

Finally Imboden said, "General, this has been a hard day on you." Lee responded, "Yes, it has been a sad day for us. I never saw troops behave more magnificently than Pickett's division of Virginians did today in that grand charge. . . . And if they had been supported as they were to have been—we would have held the position, and the day would have been ours."[1]

Lee spoke as though he were in agony. "Too bad, too bad! Oh, too bad."

General Lee spoke of the officers and men who had fallen. He mentioned Armistead, Kemper, and Garnett. Looking at Imboden he said, "We must now get back to Virginia. As many of our poor wounded as possible must be taken home." Imboden was assigned the task of forming a wagon train and transporting the wounded back to the Virginia shore opposite Williamsport, Maryland.[2]

1

While R. E. Lee pondered the fate of the Army of Northern Virginia, weary soldiers were lying down trying to sleep. Campfires were prohibited in many areas, due to the close proximity of the enemy. Soldiers whispered in subdued tones as they were seeking to analyze what had happened on the fields in Pennsylvania. Perhaps the tone of the talks and pall of gloom descending on the Confederate army are summarized by members of the Stonewall Brigade, camped on Culp's Hill, northeast of Gettysburg. They missed "Mighty Stonewall." In their opinion, the battle had been one of lost opportunities. One soldier said, "The plain truth . . . or the matter is this: Lee blundered; Stuart blundered; Longstreet, Ewell and Pickett blundered. . . . The whole campaign was a blunder."[3]

John Imboden

National Archives

After a short nap, Jed Hotchkiss arose at 2:00 a.m. He began work on the maps that would take the army to the Potomac River. He learned that his friend, Major John Harman, had been ordered to guide Lieutenant General Richard S. Ewell's wagon train through the mountain pass west of Fairfield. Ewell told Harman, "Get the train safely across the Potomac, or I never want to see your face again."[4]

There was work to be done on the "Glorious Fourth." A truce was declared to bury the dead and to treat the wounded. Troops roaming the battlefield were presented with appalling scenes. The dead had been cut down as though a farmer had cut wheat to be bound in sheaves. The blackened, bloated bodies of man and beast were everywhere. Bodies were found by fences, behind rocks and trees, wherever the battle had raged. Many had their last human expression frozen on their face. Some had smiles, others had a grimace. One veteran said, "They lay in great winnows on the ground. . . . Barns and houses were crowded with wounded men. . . . They were in cow and horse stalls, in the loft and hay mow."[5] It was a scene to make the most resolute retch, and hurry back to their lines. Those who walked among the dead and wounded had no appetite. There was also a smell in the air, almost bittersweet: the stench of death.

Both Lee and Meade had lost key lieutenants. Meade, particularly missed the presence of the dead John Reynolds, as well as both the badly wounded Winfield Scott Hancock and John Gibbon from the II Corps. Lee was also running low on ammunition and other badly needed supplies.

Some of the residents of Gettysburg had noted a gloom setting in after Pickett's Charge. They awoke on Saturday morning, and found that Confederate troops had withdrawn from positions near the northern edge of town. David Kendlehart, along with his sons John and William, felt General Meade should be made aware of the withdrawal.

As they sought Meade, they met George Arnold, a local banker, who informed them that it was impossible to get through the Union lines. Kendlehart would not be deterred. Meeting some of the officers, he was taken to Meade's headquarters and relayed the information. Supposedly this was the first news Meade had concerning the pull back of the rebel lines.[6]

Early in the morning, Marsena Patrick rode into Gettysburg. Later in the day, he found that Meade had been forced to move his headquarters from the home of Widow Leister. The reason, the piles of dead horses around the house. In the afternoon, he sought shelter from the heavy rain in the barn. To his surprise it was vacant. Patrick thought it was the only barn in the area not in use as a hospital. The Union troops were hungry, and rations had not arrived from Westminster. Patrick was sure the battle was over, but he was just as sure that Meade was in no position to attack Lee.[7]

There was a shower in the morning, but in the afternoon, the heavens opened. In the low-lying areas, waters rose rapidly. Some of the wounded and equipment had to be moved quickly to higher ground. Rain as it might, the waters could not wash away the hurt of the bruised men, broken families, and the loss of young men killed on the field of battle.

Rufus Dawes of the 6th Wisconsin wrote to loved ones:

> I am entirely safe through the first three of these terrible days of this bloody struggle. The fighting has been the most desperate I ever saw. On July 1st, our corps was thrown in front, unsupported and almost annihilated. My regiment was detached from the brigade and we charged upon and captured the Second Mississippi rebel regiment. Their battle flag is now at General Meade's headquarters, inscribed as follows: Captured by the Sixth Wisconsin, together with the entire regiment, kept by Sergeant Evans for two days, while a prisoner in the hands of the enemy.

> The Sixth has lost so far one hundred and sixty men. . . . O, Mary, it is sad to look now at our shattered band of devoted men. Only four field officers in the brigade have escaped and I am one of them. I have no opportunity to say more now or to write to any one else. Tell mother I am safe. There is no chance to telegraph.

> God has been kind to me and I think he will spare me.

> What a solemn birthday. My little band, now only two hundred men, have all been out burying the bloody corpse of friend and foe. No fighting today. Both armies need rest from the exhaustion of the desperate struggle. My

boys until just now have had nothing to eat since yesterday morning. No regiment in this army or in any other army in the world ever did better service than ours. We were detached from the brigade early on the first day and we operated as an independent command. I saved my men all I could and we suffered terribly to be sure, but less than any other regiment in the brigade. We captured a regiment. I don't know as we will get our credit before the country, but we have it with our Generals.

I went in person taking the captured battle flag to General Meade, at headquarters of the Army of the Potomac. The object of this visit was to obtain, if possible, permission to send the battle flag to the Governor of Wisconsin to be retained at the capitol of Wisconsin as a trophy. In this effort I was unsuccessful, and I brought the flag back. As I passed along from General Meade's headquarters to Culp's Hill, carrying the rebel flag loosely folded over my arm, I took my course over the ground where General Pickett made his charge. Many wounded Confederate soldiers were still lying on this ground. A badly wounded Confederate sergeant who had lain upon the ground during the night, called to me in a faint voice: "You have got our flag!" It was a sergeant of the Second Mississippi regiment. The men of this regiment who had escaped from the railroad cut and other casualties in July first, had taken part in this attack. This man informed me that the commander of his regiment at the time of its surrender was Major John A. Blair. . . .[8]

The "Glorious Fourth" was a special day for Rufus Dawes, he was celebrating his 25th birthday.[9]

Oliver Norton, a member of the 83rd Pennsylvania, and the V Corps, also wrote home, seeking to assure his loved ones that he was safe. Oliver told his sister that Colonel Strong Vincent had been mortally wounded. Vincent asked Norton how "The boys had fought. . . ." His eyes brightened as Oliver told how the 83rd, the 20th Maine, and other units in the brigade had fought fiercely to save Little Round Top and had emerged victorious. Vincent smiled weakly.[10]

William Powell, another member of the V Corps, later surveyed the battlefield before the rains came. He was lavish in his praise of surgeons who worked day and night ministering to the wounded. Their coats were off, sleeves rolled up to the elbows, and hands and aprons bloody. Nursing attendants wiped their brows and stuffed food in their mouths even as they performed surgery.[11]

Powell quickly moved on. Bodies were torn in every conceivable manner. There were piles of arms and legs. Internal organs protruded through open flesh in the stomach and side. "We saw the horrors of war, enough to make the heart ache and revolt at the inhumanity of man to man."[12] The surgeons were very humane, the doctors of both armies treating the blue and gray alike.

For days, more young men from the North and South were added to the long list of those giving their "last full measure of devotion" at Gettysburg. Powell never forgot the burial parties.

> There were so many . . . It seemed a gigantic task. Sometimes a grave was dug beside where the body lay, and it was merely turned over into a narrow pit. Sometimes long trenches were dug, . . . one corpse after another was laid in; then the earth was thrown back, making a long ridge of fresh ground. Whenever names could be ascertained, each grave was marked by a headboard with name and regiment of the dead soldier. All these dead, so rapidly consigned to the earth, were living men but yesterday, or the day before, in full vigor of manhood. We had seen many of them marching in their youthful prime.[13]

News traveled slowly in those days. The Army of the Potomac had not yet heard about Grant's victory at Vicksburg. On the field, in the Army of the Potomac, the fourth meant more than ever. There was quiet gratitude, but little rejoicing because there was so much death and destruction. Soldiers, young and old, thanked God that the battle was over, and they fervently hoped it would not be renewed.[14]

The 149th New York Infantry awoke to the realization that "the enemy has skedaddled, and we are master of the field." Yet when they walked over the battlefield, the sights "made the men sick in body and mind." They saw the price of victory. "The havoc in the Union lines was terrible, but among the enemy it was still more so."[15]

For three days, the Confederates had attacked the Union lines. Now the soldiers of the Army of Northern Virginia wondered if Meade would attack them. The Confederates knew they "were frightfully extended, bleeding, and almost without ammunition."[16] The longer Lee stayed, the greater the risk to his army.

Pete Longstreet was in a reflective mood. The armies rested on the fourth, one under the bright laurels secured by the brave work of the day before, but in profound sorrow over the silent forms of the host of comrades who had fallen during those three fateful days, whose blood bathed the thirsty fields of Gettysburg. . . . While gentle rain came to mellow the sod that marked the honored rest of friend and foe alike. . . . There was nothing left for the vanquished but to march for distant homeward lines."[17]

The Duke of Wellington once said, "Nothing except a battle lost can be half so melancholy as a battle won."[18] Death, destruction, and desolation prevailed on the morning of July 4, 1863, in Pennsylvania.

The first half of the day was spent burying the dead, and collecting firearms and implements of war scattered over the far-flung battlefield.

After working on his maps during the early hours of the fourth, Jed Hotchkiss "took a fine sleep" during the late morning. There was a heavy shower while he slept. Richard S. Ewell was staying on the Cashtown Road, but "everything was moving by the Fairfield Road."[19]

South of Gettysburg, wagons were coming and going from Westminster, Maryland. Herman Haupt had established the Union supply base in this Carroll County town. Trains brought supplies to the village. They were unloaded, placed in wagons, and headed north to Gettysburg. At the same time, wagons bringing prisoners and the wounded from Gettysburg were arriving in Westminster. Among the wounded were Major Generals Winfield Scott Hancock and John Gibbon. They were from the II Corps which had repulsed Pickett's charge. Some of the residents took pity upon the wounded of both armies, giving them pies and biscuits. The wounded were then placed in rambling boxcars and sent to Baltimore. The Confederates were headed for Point Lookout in southern Maryland. During the next years, more POWs would die there than the infamous Andersonville.

At Gettysburg and elsewhere those who had fallen at Gettysburg were being buried. On July 1, John Fulton Reynolds, the commander of the Union I Corps, was killed in action west of Gettysburg. On this birthday of the United States, a car from the Pennsylvania Railroad carried his body to Lancaster for burial. The church bells throughout the city tolled "a mournful requiem for the lamented brave."

Governor Curtin was unable to attend but he sent a telegram.

> As a General, the whole nation honors and mourns him, but Pennsylvania has reasons to cherish with especial pride, alike the noble qualities of character which led him to his high command, and his chivalric character on the historic battleground where he closed his life so gloriously.[20]

The Reynolds' family was grief stricken by the death of the general. So was a young woman by the name of Katherine Hewitt. As Major William Riddle examined the general's body after he had fallen, he found a small Catholic medal dangling from a chain around the general's neck. On the back were the words, "dear Kate." But who was Kate, where was she?

The family did not have to wait long for an answer. On Friday morning, July 3, there was a request from a Miss Hewitt to view the body of General Reynolds. The family granted the request and met the young woman. Ellie and Hal were very much impressed, "she seemed to be a superior person," Jeane wrote.

> During the conversation, Kate said she had met John Reynolds in California where she had been serving as a governess for a San Francisco family. Their friendship soon developed into a long-range romance. They had discussed marriage, but at John's request, they were keeping their love secret until after the war, if John survived, they would announce their plans, marry, and honeymoon in Europe. If John did not survive, then Kate would enter a convent. She declared that life without John Reynolds, had no meaning for her. Now her plans, hopes, and dreams were shattered. What was true for Katherine Hewitt held true for thousands in the North and South.[21]

Riding in the rain were troopers of John Buford's cavalry command. They had participated in the fighting on July 1, and then had been sent to Westminster to protect the army supply base. Now they were on the road to Frederick in an effort to gain the rear of Lee's line and cut him off his retreat.

Another man was on the road, traveling alone. His name was Charles Carleton Coffin, a noted war correspondent. He rode twenty miles in the driving rain, covering the distance in two and one-half hours. The military had the telegraph tied up in Westminster, so there was nothing to do but travel on. Coffin hopped a train to Baltimore, and then another to New York. There he locked himself in a room, and then telegraphed the story to the *Boston Journal*. The next day his account of Gettysburg brought added joy to the citizens of the North.

About 4:00 p.m., Luther Hopkins, a member of the 6th Virginia Cavalry, heard "a low rumbling sound . . . resembling distant thunder, except that it was continuous."[22]

Rain was falling, and there was thunder and lightning, nature's fireworks, but the sound arose above the storm. Hopkins says, "we saw a long line of wagons with their white covers moving along the Chambersburg Road." As the men saw the wagons taking the roads from Gettysburg, they got the message. The Army of Northern Virginia was in retreat. This was the first time they had known defeat. The rumble of the wagons sounded like thunder.

In his report to the government authorities in Richmond, Robert E. Lee stated:

> The army remained at Gettysburg during the 4th, and at night began to retire by the road to Fairfield, carrying with it about 4,000 prisoners. Nearly 2,000 had previously been paroled, but the enemy's numerous wounded that had fallen into our hands after the first and second days' engagement were left behind.

> Owing to the strength of the enemy's position and the reduction of our ammunition, a renewal of the engagement could not be hazarded, and the difficulty of procuring supplies rendered it almost impossible to continue where we were. . . .

> Little progress was made (the night of the 4th) owing to a severe storm which greatly embarrassed our movements. The rear of the column did not leave its position near Gettysburg until after daylight on the 5th.[23]

Two British observers traveled with the Army of Northern Virginia from Gettysburg. Lawley visited army headquarters, where he learned that the Confederate Army would begin to march on the roads from Gettysburg when evening came. The shortage of ammunition, plus an expected Union buildup were listed as the two biggest reasons. The ordnance and wagons with wounded would travel via Cashtown Pass, while the rest of the wagons, plus the cattle taken in Pennsylvania, would travel by the Fairfield Road.

On the morning of the Fourth, Colonel James Fremantle had a long talk with his friend, William Nelson Pendleton. Later in the day, Fremantle talked with General Longstreet. The General said the mistake was in not concentrating the Army of Northern Virginia, and that 12,500 men were not enough to penetrate Union lines. Thirty thousand men should have been used in the assault.[24]

Jeb Stuart was also riding in the rain this "Glorious Fourth." General Lee had detailed Stuart to guard the left flank of the Army of Northern Virginia. Troopers under the command of Albert Jenkins and Chambliss were to ride with Stuart. Colonel W. W. Blackford rode on ahead to scout the area around Emmitsburg. It was rumored that the Yankees were in possession of the town. Indeed, Judson Kilpatrick was already in the area.

Stuart passed to the right of the army and headed south. The rain made things worse, and it was symbolic of the feelings and the tears that would flow when relatives North and South learned the fate of loved ones who had fallen at Gettysburg. After a while, the heavy rain forced Stuart to call a halt.

By now the long train of Confederate wounded was underway, heading toward Cashtown, the mountains, the Potomac River, and safety. John Imboden describes the agony and the difficulty of the wagon train of wounded:

> Shortly after noon the very windows of heaven seemed to have been opened. Rain fell in dashing torrents, and in a little while the whole face of the earth was covered with water. The meadows became small lakes, raging streams ran across the road in ever depression of the ground. The storm increased in fury every moment, canvas was no protection against it, and the poor wounded lying upon the hard, naked boards of the wagon—bodies were drenched by the cold rain. Horses and mules were blinded and maddened by the storm and became almost unmanageable. The roar of the winds and waters made it almost impossible to communicate orders; night was rapidly approaching and there was danger that in darkness the confusion would become "worse confounded."

> About 4:00 p.m. the head of the column was put in motion and begun the ascent of the mountain. The train was seventeen miles long when drawn out on the road. It was moving rapidly and from every wagon issued wails of agony. For four hours, I galloped along, passing to the front and heard more—it was too dark to see—of the horrors of war than I had witnessed from the battle of Bull Run to that day. In the wagons were men wounded and mutilated in every conceivable way. Some had their legs shattered by a shell or Minie-ball some were shot in the face, or jagged piece of shell had lacerated their heads.

> Scarcely one in hundred had received adequate surgical aid; and many had been without food for thirty-six hours.

Their ragged, dirty, and bloody clothes, all clotted and hardened with blood, were rasping the tender, inflamed lips of the gaping wounds. Very few of the wagons had even straw in them, and all were without springs. The road was rough and rocky. The jolting was enough to have killed strong, sound men. From nearly every wagon as the horses trotted along such cries and shrieks as these greeted the ears:

"My God! Will no one have mercy and kill me, and end my misery?"

"O God! Why can't I die?"

"Oh! Stop one minute, take me out and leave me by the roadside to die."

"I am dying! Oh, my poor wife and children! What will become of you?"

Some were praying, others were uttering the most fearful oaths and imprecations that despair could wiring from them in their agony.

Occasionally a wagon would be passed from which only low, deep moans and groans could be heard.

No help could be given to any of the suffers. On, on we must move on.

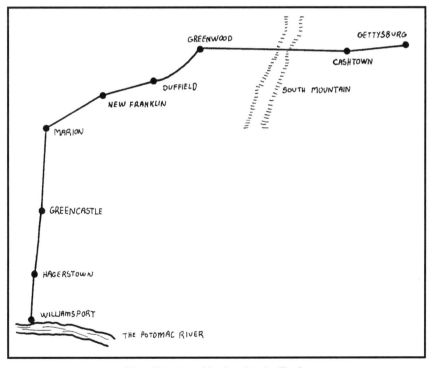

The Route of Imboden's Train

Gary Fornwalt

The storms continued and the darkness was fearful. There was no time even to fill a canteen with water for a dying man; for, except the drivers and guards, disposed in compact bodies every half mile, all were wounded in that vast train of human misery.

No language can convey an idea of the horrors of the most horrible of all nights of our long and bloody war.[25]

Cashtown was the first village to witness the Confederate wagon train of misery. For the rest of the Army of Northern Virginia, the artillery, infantry, and supply wagons, the route would be to Fairfield or Millerstown. Nearly 50,000 soldiers and thousands of animals would pass through the village during the next twenty-four hours.

The village had been settled by Squire Miller in 1755. He was the largest landowner and plotted the town. His large home became a stagecoach stop and inn. As the Confederate army marched by on July 5, the owners of the inn provided hot bean soup to the drenched rebel soldiers.

On July 3, an unheralded clash occurred near Fairfield. It involved the 6th Virginia Cavalry and the 6th U.S. Cavalry. The men in blue were turned back. However, had they been successful, they could have cut off Lee's line of retreat.

The downpour quickly turned the roads into a quagmire. The rain pelted man and beast. Those in Imboden's wagons had little shelter, and those remaining in the field hospitals had the barest of shelters. Many of the field hospitals had been established close to streams so there would be a supply of water to quench the thirst of the suffering. By late afternoon, the medical attendants had to take the wounded to higher ground, and sought buildings of any type to use as hospitals.

Preparations continued for the departure of the Confederate infantry. The wagon park at Black Horse Tavern on the Fairfield Road was a beehive of activity. The wagon park at Bream's Mill on Marsh Run was also busy.

During the heavy rain, the British observers, Lawley and Fremantle, entered the tent of James Longstreet. The general said that the lack of ammunition was one of the reasons for the retreat. Apparently, Lee had but one day's supply left. Fremantle noted that the Fairfield Road resembled the beginning of a large cattle drive. There were horses, mules, and cattle everywhere. The cattle had been rounded up during Confederate visits to the prosperous farms of Pennsylvania. They would accompany Ewell's wagon train, and provide food for the Army of Northern Virginia.

Seeking shelter from the driving rain was another group of soldiers. They were the Union prisoners of war, gathered along the Fairfield Road and waiting the long trek to Virginia. They were being guarded by the survivors of Pickett's Division. Lee had proposed an exchange of prisoners so he could be relieved of the burden. Meade denied the request.

THE THIRD CORPS—CSA

By flickering light in the tent of A. P. Hill, the retreat on the roads from Gettysburg had been planned. It was agreed the night of the third, that unless Meade assumed the offensive, the "Third Corps which had suffered most heavily should lead the retreat after dark on Saturday, July 4."[26]

James Lane's brigade led the procession in the midst of a driving rain. The route was the Fairfield Road.

The road was not macadamized. Ewell's wagon train, which had begun leaving around 3:00 p.m. or 4:00 p.m., had carved deep ruts into "the muddy surface rendering it almost impassable." The soldiers, acquired a new coat, not of snow, but of mud.[27] Their clothing looked horrible.

Meanwhile, the Union cavalry, led by Judson Kilpatrick, started south before the heavy rain began. By the time they reached Emmitsburg, the roads had become very muddy and difficult to negotiate.

The Union cavalry halted momentarily in Emmitsburg, and headed west toward Fountaindale on the road to Waynesboro. Darkness came early, and the column of horsemen had to contend with the blackness of night. Steep embankments on both sides of the road allowed only four horsemen to ride abreast. "The night was not fit for man or beast."

Kilpatrick's column, being mounted, was able to make better time than Ewell's wagon train. The men in blue narrowed the gap, though they were wet, tired and miserable.

The Confederate guard, mainly the 1st Maryland and 4th North Carolina, had placed a piece of artillery in Monterey Gap near the hotel of the same name. The cannon commanded the road. On either side were skirmishers, many of them sharpshooters. The men in gray had been ordered to make a strong defense at this spot to protect the wagon train that was not far away. With the firing of the cannon, the Confederate riflemen poured forth a volley. The 5th Michigan was in the advance and thus took the shots. But there was no place to go. They could not turn around. For a moment it was like a hopeless traffic jam.

Luther Hopkins said the night had already been hideous in nature. Some of the captured cattle with the Confederate train got loose on the mountain. "They were constantly bellowing. The noise of the animals coupled with the thunder and flashes of lightning were bad enough. Then came the Union attack." Added to the night scene were the sights and sounds of battle, shouts of surprise, pistols firing, and other noises. It was a nightmare.[28]

The Union cavalry dismounted and fought as skirmishers. Men became trapped in thickets. Each man was on his own, and most fell several times on the slippery slopes of the mountain.

The Second Brigade of Kilpatrick's cavalry, commanded by George Custer, had been engaged for an hour. Major Charles Capehart of the First West Virginia was ordered to report to General Kilpatrick. Capehart was

instructed to reinforce Custer. Upon reporting to Custer, Capehart was ordered to charge the wagon train and capture it.

The officers and men were informed of their task, and "with a whoop
and yell dashed upon the train. The night was of inky darkness; nothing
was discernible a half dozen paces ahead." The West Virginians along
with forty men of the 1st Ohio Cavalry assisted the West Virginians. "Hand
to hand conflict ensued. The scene was wild and desolating," very rugged.

The wagon train covered a distance of eight miles. The Confederates used the underbrush along the side of the road for concealment and
for firing positions.

Many after action reports are quite glowing. Such was the case with
W. E. Crumble Jones, a Confederate cavalry general. He states that for
more than two hours, "less than 50 men kept thousands in check." Then he
notes that "the enemy driven to desperation resorted to a charge of cavalry
that swept everything before it. . . . Horses, wagons, straggling infantrymen
and camp followers were hurled down the mountain in one confused mass."

Jones himself was in a desperate situation. He had bcome separated
from his staff and couriers. Friend and foe mingled in the darkness. General Jones "made through the fields and byways for Williamsport," seeking
to avoid capture or to be useful "as the occasion might require."[29]

The last hours of the "Glorious Fourth" brought fireworks on the mountain. Both Union and Confederate forces had to await the dawn to assess
victory or defeat.

Adding to the human misery at Monterey Pass, there was also tragedy for the animals. The pass was narrow and steep. In the tumult of battle,
several wagons, along with horses and mules, went over the side of the
mountain and plummeted to the bottom of the ravine. Most of them remained in the pit until morning. By the time they were discovered it was
too late. The poor animals died a slow horrible death from their injuries, or
from thrashing around seeking to escape the harness. Some of the drivers
also went over the side. A few were able to jump to safety. With the noises
of the night and the battle, those in the pass did not hear the agony of the
animals, or the cries of the drivers. Adding to the problems, there was no
real way to rescue the animals.

In his official report, George Custer noted that the 1st Michigan suffered heavy losses at Monterey Pass, while the 5th and 6th Michigan suffered but little. After the troops disengaged, Kilpatrick burned most of the
wagons captured from Ewell's trains. The men took what they could carry
and use.[30]

There are three epics in the story of the Gettysburg Campaign. (1)
The first involves the approach march on the roads to Gettysburg, (2) the
struggles on Seminary and Cemetery Ridges, and (3) the roads from
Gettysburg. Several markers in towns and villages describe the advance
to Pennsylvania. The battlefield is extremely well marked with monuments

and plaques. Yet only four markers are devoted to the roads from Gettysburg. Fittingly the first is on the Fairfield Road. It reads:

> The Confederate Army, the afternoon on July 4, 1863, began an orderly retreat by this road to the Potomac which they crossed the night of July 13, after delay caused by high water.

Other markers are in Funkstown, at Monterey, Falling Waters and Jones's Crossroads.

BUFORD'S CAVALRY—USA

The nation owed a great debt to John Buford and his cavalry. The troopers contested the Confederate advance on the morning of July 1, fighting bravely for time until Union infantry could arrive. Buford proudly wrote:

> The zeal, brave bravery and good humor of the officers and men on the night of June 30 and July 1 were commendable in the extreme. A heavy task was before us; we were equal to it, and shall all remember with pride that at Gettysburg we did our country much service.[31]

When the Army of the Potomac formed a line of battle on Cemetery Ridge on July 1, Winfield Scott Hancock placed Buford and his cavalry on

the left flank. There they remained until the night of July 2 when the division was ordered to Taneytown. The next day, the command proceeded to Westminster to guard the large Union supply depot that had been established by Herman Haupt.

On the "Glorious Fourth" the division was ordered to Westminster then Frederick, with the objective of moving on Williamsport with the idea of cutting off Lee's line of retreat. The cavalry reached Frederick late in the day.[32]

John Buford

Library of Congress

—2—
𝔄 ℜainy 𝔖unday

Judson Kilpatrick and Ewell's wagon train were not the only persons on the road this cold, rainy Sunday. John Imboden departed Gettysburg via the Chambersburg Pike at 4:00 p.m. on Saturday. Given the task of getting the wounded back to the Potomac, Robert E. Lee had instructed the general not to contact him until Imboden reached the safety of Winchester, and then to seek further orders. Imboden with 2,100 men and about 23 guns had the task of transporting somewhere between 12,000 and 15,000 wounded to the Potomac.

The train formed on the Cashtown Pike, between the western edge of Gettysburg and Cashtown. The storm struck before all preparations had been made. The riders had a difficult time quieting the terrified horses and mules. The canvas tops had not been put in place on all wagons. Thus the straw and the floor boards became wet, adding to the misery of the wounded.

Imboden had been instructed to take the Chambersburg Pike toward Chambersburg. However, he had discretionary orders, and once through the Cashtown Pike could take whatever road he deemed necessary.

The wagon train got underway, heading west, retracing the route of the Confederate First and Third Corps and Robert E. Lee to the fields of Gettysburg. They journeyed through Cashtown, and the wet animals, blinded and soaked by the driving rain, pulled their burdens up the mountains. Even in the twilight, it was difficult for man and beast to see.

Officers and men in the wagons were pelted with rain. There was no distinction in rank in Imboden's train this rainy night. Officers and men alike suffered from the jolting, jarring journey. The floor of the wagon was wet, and the driving rain blew water in upon the wounded. They were cold, wet, and miserable.

A member of the 16th North Carolina was able to secure a place on a bale of hay. He describes the trip:

> When we reached the top of the mountain, . . . it got very dark, but there
> was no halt made, a steady trot being kept up all night. I could never tell

14

you how we got along without some accident. During the night we passed Thad Stevens Iron Works, which Ewell's troops had burned as they passed on some days before, and they were still smoking.[1]

A few more miles, and Imboden turned the train, "column south." The route continued on narrow, muddy roads on the Pine Stump Road, through New Guilford, New Franklin, Marion, and thence to Greencastle.

Jacob Snyder farmed along the route of the train. His farm was near New Franklin. He heard the rumbling of the wagons during the night. He opened his front door, and in moments his spacious hallway was full of soldiers, shaking raindrops from their ponchos. The porch and front yard were filled with walking wounded begging for water and food, for something hot to warm them from the chill of the night and the cold rain. Later, he discovered some of his cattle missing. Milton, Jacob's son, said that Confederates were burying their deceased comrades in shallow graves along the roadside. Some of the wounded remained, saying they could no longer continue. They would take their chances in captivity. He said, "I shall never forget those ghastly wounds, and the thousands of faces, dusky with powder."[2]

Along the route were broken down wagons, disabled by broken axles, wheel problems, or other failures. Often the horse-drawn vehicles became stuck in the mud, sometimes, to the axle hub. Drivers beat and cursed the horses and mules urging them to exert extra effort in pulling.

Henry Hege, another farmer, living along the train of misery's route, said the wounded groaned at every jerk of the wagon. Some of the mounted escort left the column and road to nearby farms seeking to confiscate farm wagons to replace the ones that were broken.

About 4:00 a.m. on this rainy Sunday, Rev. J. C. Smith, living at the edge of Greencastle, heard the rumble of the wagons. At first, he thought it might be Confederate reinforcements headed north. However, the column was headed south. Smith noted, even in the darkness, the startling contrast from a week earlier. As the Confederates had marched northward, they were boasting of capturing Harrisburg and Philadelphia, and striking a blow to end the war. Now it was over, and they were in retreat.[3]

Smith noted that those wounded in the lower extremities were placed in wagons, while those wounded above the waist were forced to walk in the rain and mud. Cold compresses were placed on the inflamed wounds. Clothes were used to catch the falling rain water. The exposed wounds were hideous. "No one, with any feelings of pity, will ever want to see such a sight even once in a lifetime."[4]

John Imboden felt that despite the rigors of the stormy night, the darkness had been his ally, saving him from harassment from enemy cavalry. He felt a little better when he reached Greencastle, knowing that he was just twelve or fifteen miles from Williamsport and the Potomac River. However, his troubles were just ready to begin.

A portion of the cavalry escort, the 18th Virginia, had proceeded about a mile beyond Greencastle. Then came an attack, not by Union troopers, but from thirty or forty residents of Greencastle. Armed with axes, they cut the spokes of ten or twelve wagons in the "train of misery. . . ." The moment Imboden learned of the attack, he sent a detachment of cavalry to capture every citizen "who had been engaged in this work, and treat them as prisoners of war."[5] This stopped the trouble for the moment, but at every crossroads there was harassment from Union cavalry.

Just south of Greencastle, the Williamsport-Greencastle Turnpike branched off to the right. It ran several miles west of Hagerstown, to the Potomac. Imboden took this route (current Route 63).

Another of the Union assaults occurred at Cunningham's Crossroads, or modern day Cearfoss, south of Greencastle. Approximately two hundred fifty Union troopers were involved. Fire from McClanahan's Confederate battery helped to drive them away. However, some of the Union troopers persisted in their attacks for miles. When the lead elements of Imboden's train entered Williamsport, the tail of the column was just leaving Marion, Pennsylvania, seventeen miles away.

Some of these hit-and-run attacks were led by a Captain Pierce and members of the 12th New York Cavalry. As the last elements of Imboden's train left Greencastle, they came under attack from the troopers of Irvin Gregg's Union cavalry riding from Chambersburg.

Imboden's plight was serious. The Confederate infantry was hours and miles away. He was unsure where the Rebel cavalry was, and certain the enemy was nearby.

> Our situation was frightful. We had probably ten thousands animals and nearly all the wagons of General Lee's army under our charge, and all the wounded, . . . that could be brought from Gettysburg. Our supply of provisions consisted of a wagon-load of flour, . . . a small lot of fat cattle which I had collected in Pennsylvania on my way to Gettysburg, and some sugar and coffee procured in the same way at Mercersburg.[6]

John Imboden's back was not just to the wall, it was to the river. He ran the risk of being overwhelmed, and with Lee's escape route being cut, his situation was indeed desperate.

The 21st Virginia reached Williamsport ahead of Imboden. They had been assigned the task of guarding prisoners and stragglers.

They crossed the Potomac on the fifth and seized some flour which they brought to Williamsport in a captured wagon. They also purchased some bacon in the town as well as a Dutch oven.

They were present when the immense wagon train began arriving late on the fifth. At last the jolting wagons could stop, safe for the moment. For those wounded in the train, the trip "had been sheer agony."

Imboden found new problems in the Maryland town on the banks of the river. Union troops from Frederick had destroyed the pontoon bridge several miles downstream at Falling Waters. And with two days of heavy rain the Potomac was rising rapidly. Flood stage had been reached, and that meant the ford was impassable.

A light rain was also falling this Sunday morning in Gettysburg. At dawn, Stuart and his troopers headed south, endeavoring to protect the left flank of the Confederate army. He stopped for a few moments in Emmitsburg to study maps, to feed the horses, and to rest. He wanted to head for Cavetown west of the mountains, but learned that a large Union column had taken the route he wished to follow. Jeb captured sixty or seventy Yankees and some Union supplies.

Stuart then took the Old Frederick Road and led his column south. His destination was Cooperstown, as he called it, known by the residents as Creagarstown. En route, some of his men wound up in the Moravian village of Graceham.

Belva Ann Elizabeth Cramer was a little girl in the summer of 1863. Her parents, Mr. and Mrs. William Cramer, operated the general store in the picturesque village of Graceham, east of Thurmont.

The Cramers thought they were safe. Union infantry had gone through the village on June 29. Thus they were shocked when Jeb Stuart and the Confederate cavalry rode into the village. Mr. Cramer did not have time to hide his horses or the black gunpowder that he kept in stock.

In front of the store was a big pump. The Confederate troopers and their mounts were thirsty. Belva pumped and pumped water for them. She had a bad tooth and the vigorous exercise increased her pain. As the tears rolled down her cheeks, a trooper said, "Don't cry little girl. We're dirty and ragged, but we are gentlemen and we will not hurt you."[7]

Jeb Stuart, the Confederate cavalry chieftain, was plagued with problems throughout the Gettysburg campaign. On June 28, he captured a large Union wagon train at Rockville. Instead of destroying it, Jeb took the train with him, thus slowing his progress, and robbing General Lee of vital information. Union cavalry under Judson Kilpatrick and George Custer blocked his path at Hanover, necessitating a detour to Carlisle farther north.

Judson Kilpatrick

Library of Congress

Now his problem was getting across the Catoctin Mountains and rejoining Lee and the rest of the Army of Northern Virginia in Washington County, Maryland, west of the mountain.

He learned that another Union force, some of Wesley Merritt's troopers, were in possession of Harman's Pass, the road leading from Mechanicstown (Thurmont) to Smithsburg (current Route 77). Another detour was needed.

At this point, one can only speculate as to Stuart's exact route to rejoin the main body of the Confederate army. Most scholars feel that he rode northwest from Cregerston to the hamlet of Franklinville on the Emmitsburg Road, striking the Hampton Valley Road into Eyler's Valley, then continuing northwesterly to Deerfield. There, according to John Winters and elderly residents, Stuart took a logging trail through the mountain.

In his official report, Stuart tells of stopping in Cooperstown (Creagarstown) to feed the fatigued and famished horses. He tells of going through Harbaugh Valley by Zion Church. When he emerged from the mountain late in the afternoon, the road in his front led to Smithtown (Smithsburg) and the other to Leitersburg. He found the enemy, Kilpatrick, in force. Stuart ordered his troopers to dismount. The rebel cavalry had to "fight from crag to crag to dislodge the enemy."[8]

George A. Custer

Kilpatrick reports that he had placed horse artillery and a brigade of cavalry on three hills commanding the approaches to Smithsburg. The Union general says it was 5:00 p.m. when the rebel columns emerged from the mountain passes. Half an hour later, Fuller's battery opened fire, followed a few moments later by Elder's battery. Kilpatrick then says that in less than one hour Stuart was in retreat.[9] It seems as though Kilpatrick broke off, and even sent a message to General William French in Frederick for support. Later, he received a reprimand from Alfred Pleasonton, the Union cavalry commander, for making the appeal to an infantry officer rather than going through him.

Roger Keller, author of *The Events in Washington County During the Civil War*, feels this was a gross mistake. Kilpatrick broke off the engagement without knowledge of

Stuart's strength. By concluding the action, Kilpatrick left the route of the Confederate infantry to the Potomac open, as well as Stuart's route to Hagerstown. This seems to be a far more serious error than any committed by Meade on the roads from Gettysburg. By moving to Hagerstown, Kilpatrick would have been between the Potomac River and Lee's infantry and cavalry.[10] Kilpatrick's command went into camp north of Boonsboro about midnight. On Monday, he conferred with John Buford about the course of action. It was agreed that Kilpatrick would harass Lee from Hagerstown, while Buford would attempt to strike Confederate positions at Williamsport.

While Kilpatrick was riding on what is now Maryland 66 to Boonsboro, night was falling. Stuart, desiring to know the location of the rest of the Army of Northern Virginia, "sent a trusty and intelligent soldier, Private Robert W. Goode, 1st Virginia Cavalry, to look for General Lee.[11] Goode returned with vital information in the morning.

Meanwhile, Colonel Addison W. Preston with the 1st Vermont Cavalry had arrived at Leitersburg. There he had captured 100 Rebels, a large herd of cattle and many wagons. He and his men rode into Hagerstown where he made camp. Preston and his men had not eaten nor slept in thirty-six hours. The 1st Vermont remained in Hagerstown until the approach of Albert Jenkins the next morning. Then the command proceeded to Boonsboro and joined the rest of Kilpatrick's cavalry.

SECOND CORPS—CSA

Shortly after dark on the fourth, the infantry began to move on the roads from Gettysburg. For many it was a case of "hurry up and wait." Daylight came, then mid morning arrived, and still the First and Third Corps were not underway. Thus, R. S. Ewell says it was almost noon before the Second Corps began moving on the Fairfield Road. The march was six to eight miles, depending upon the beginning of the march. Union cavalry kept nipping at the Confederate rear like a hound after its prey.

Jubal Early's division arose at 2:00 a.m. Their task was to act as the rear guard for Ewell's Second Corps. John Gordon's brigade was the last in line, followed by Lige White's cavalry. Early found a traffic jam in Fairfield caused by too many wagons. Then came a message from White saying that the Yankees were coming. Early threatened to use blank ammunition to sort out the wagon mess. When Union troops came close to Gordon's lines they were met with artillery and small arms fire, and halted. Gordon's men then spent the night at Fairfield.[12]

Colonel Fremantle also speaks of the beginning of the march:

5th July (Sunday)—The night was very bad—thunder and lightning, torrents of rain—the road knee-deep in mud and water, and often blocked up with wagons "come to grief." I pitied the wretched plight of the unfortunate soldiers who were to follow us. Our progress was naturally very slow indeed, and we took eight hours to go as many miles.

At 8 a.m. we halted a little beyond the village of Fairfield, near the entrance to a mountain pass. No sooner had we done so and lit a fire, than an alarm was spread that Yankee cavalry were upon us. Several shots flew over our heads, but we never could discover from whence they came.

News also arrived of the capture of the whole of Ewell's beautiful wagons. These reports created a regular stampede amongst the wagoners, and Longstreet's drivers started off as fast as they could go. Our medical trio, however, firmly declined to budge, and came to this wise conclusion, partly urged by the pangs of hunger, and partly from the consideration that, if the Yankee cavalry did come, the crowded state of the road in our rear would prevent our escape. Soon afterwards, some Confederate cavalry were pushed to the front, who cleared the pass after a slight skirmish.[13]

While Early's men held Fairfield, the First Corps had plodded on during the day, reaching the crest of the mountain. The first portion of their retreat from Gettysburg was complete. However, they were exhausted. It had been a difficult day. Douglas S. Freeman writes that this "'Rainy Sunday' was sixteen hours of purgatory."[14]

Harry Gilmor says Lee's army was not a defeated entity. "There was not a rout . . . and all that silly stuff we read in the Northern accounts of 'flying rebels' and shattered army are pure fictions prepared for the Northern market.[15]

When the Second Corps cleared Fairfield, they left behind severely wounded comrades—those who were too critical to be placed in Imboden's wagon train. The rain and the dampness added to the misery that they would no longer see their friends of previous days. Water and mud were knee to ankle deep on the Pennsylvania roads. A portion of the Second Corps camped within sight of the Fairfield Pass.

FIRST CORPS—CSA

John Bell Hood's Texans moved from Seminary Ridge in the early hours of Sunday morning. Progress was very slow, due to the heavy rains and high winds. About daylight, Lee had ridden through the ranks en route to Fairfield. The survivors of the attack on Little Round Top gave their commander a rousing cheer. Lee raised his hat in appreciation and rode on in silence.[16]

Kemper's Brigade spent the night at Monterey Pass.

For George Pickett and his men, it was indeed a sad march homeward. Writing to his beloved Sally, George said:

Well, it is all over now. The battle is lost, and many of us are prisoners, many are dead, many wounded, bleeding and dying. Your soldier lives and mourns and but for you, my darling, he would rather, a million times rather, be back there with his dead, to sleep for all time in an unknown grave.

On the Fourth—far from a glorious Fourth to us or to any with love for his fellowmen—I wrote you just a line of heartbreak. The sacrifice of life on the blood-soaked field on the fatal third was too awful for the heralding of victory, even for our victorious foe, who I think, believe as we do, that it decided the fate of our cause. No words can picture the anguish of that roll-call—the breathless waits between the responses. The "Here" of those who, by God's mercy, had miraculously escaped the awful rain of shot and shell was a sob—a gasp—a knell—for the unanswered name of his comrade. There was no tone of thankfulness for having been spared to answer to their names, but rather a toll, and an unvoiced wish that they, too, had been among the missing.

Even now I can hear them cheering as I gave the order, "Forward!" I can feel the thrill of their joyous voices as they called out all along the line, "We'll follow you, Marse George. We'll follow you." Oh, how faithfully they kept their word—following me on—on—to their death, and I believing in the promised support, led them on—on—on—Oh, God!

I can't write you a love letter today, my Sally, for with great love for you and my gratitude to God for sparing my life to devote to you, comes the over-powering thought of those whose lives were sacrificed—of the broken-hearted widows and mothers and orphans. The moans of my wounded boys, the sight of the dead, upturned faces, flood my soul with grief—and here am I whom they trusted, whom they followed, leaving them on that field of carnage—and guarding four thousand prisoners across the river back to Winchester. Such a duty for men who a few hours ago covered themselves with glory eternal!

Well, darling, I put the prisoners all on their honor and gave them equal liberties with my own soldier boys. My first command to them was to go and enjoy themselves the best they could, and they have obeyed my order. Today a Dutchman and two of his comrades came up to and told me that they were lost and besought me to help them find their com-rades. They had been with my men and were separated from their own comrades. So I sent old Floyd off on St. Paul to find out where they be-longed and deliver them.

This is too gloomy and too poor a letter for so beautiful a sweetheart, but it seems sacrilegious, almost to say I love you, with the hearts that are stilled to love on the field of battle.[17]

Augustus Dickert in Kershaw's Brigade describes the "Rainy Sunday" on the roads from Gettysburg:

At daylight on the morning of the fifth the remnant of the once grand army turned its face southward. I say remnant, for with the loss of near one-third its number in killed, wounded, and prisoners the pride, prestige of victory, the feelings of invincibility, were lost to the remainder, and the army was in rather ill condition when it took up the retreat. Lee has been severely criticized for fighting the battle of Gettysburg, especially the last charge of Pickett; but there are circumstances of minor import sometimes that surround a commander which force him to undertake or attempt that which his better judgment might dictate as a false step. The world judges by results the successes and achievements of a General, not by his motives or intentions.[18]

Colonel Fremantle was still in Fairfield when Ewell arrived. The British officer noted he was a rather odd-looking character, "with a bald head, a prominent nose, and a rather haggard sickly face. Ewell was still suffering from the loss of his leg at Second Manassas. Occasionally he fell from his horse." When Fremantle saw Ewell, "he was in a great state of disgust in consequence of the supposed loss of his wagons and refused to be comforted by General Lee."[19]

A. P. Hill's report of the Third Corps on the roads from Gettysburg is covered in a few short lines, saying that the troops fell back to their original lines after Pickett's charge, "and remained thus until the night of the 4th, when the march was taken up toward Hagerstown, by Fairfield and Waynesboro. At Hagerstown, we lay in line of battle from the 7th to the night of the 13th, when I moved with my corps in the direction of the pontoon bridge at Falling Waters."[20]

R. H. Anderson says on the fifth, he was "directed to hold the gaps in the mountains between Fairfield and Waynesborough. In the evening, I moved to a place called Frogtown at the base of the mountains."[21]

A. R. Wright moved from Gettysburg to Fairfield about dark. However, in the downpour it was midnight before he arrived in Millerstown. He was handed orders and told to move on to Monterey Gap to support Iverson's brigade which was under attack from the Union cavalry. At dawn, Wright came upon the rear of the train but found the road completely blocked, making further progress impossible.[22] He halted his men and permitted them to take a rest in the mud, while he went to find Iverson. The latter assured him that the danger was past. Wright directed him to move on toward Waynesboro while he held the pass. General Anderson soon arrived and assumed command.

While Hill's men were plodding on, Colonel Fremantle rejoined General Longstreet on the road to the top of the mountain. At 4:00 p.m., they stopped on the western slope of the mountain. The road forked, one heading back to Emmitsburg, the other to Hagerstown. The Colonel and Major Moses entered a farmhouse where they found several wounded Yankees, and one who had died. The lads had been wounded in the Monterey action.

The women in this house were great abolitionists. When Major Fairfax rode up, he inquired of one of them whether the corpse was that of a Confederate or Yankee (the body was in the veranda, covered with a white sheet).

The woman made a gesture with her foot, and replied, "If it was a Rebel, do you think it would be here long?" Fairfax then said, "Is it a woman who speaks in such a manner, of dead man who do no one any harm?" She thereupon colored up, and said she wasn't in earnest.

At 6 o'clock we rode on again (by the Hagerstown road), and came up with General Longstreet at 7:30. The road was full of soldiers marching in a particular lively manner—the wet and mud seemed to have produced no effect whatever on their spirits, which were passing about from company to company with many remarks upon the personal beauty of Uncle Abe. The same old chaff was going on of "Come out of that hat—I know you're in it—I see your legs a-dangling down."

When we halted for the night, skirmishing was going on in front and rear—Stuart in front and Ewell in rear. Our bivouac being near a large tavern, General Longstreet had ordered some supper there for himself and his staff; but when we went to devour it, we discovered General M'Laws and his officers rapidly finishing it. We, however, soon got more, the Pennsylvanian proprietors being particularly anxious to propitiate the General, in hopes that he would spare their livestock, which had been condemned to death by the ruthless Moses.

During supper, women came rushing in at intervals, saying—"Oh, good heavens, now they're killing our fat hogs. Which is the General? Which is the Great Officer? Our milch cows are now going." To all which expressions Longstreet replied, shaking his head in a melancholy manner— "Yes, madam, it's very sad—very sad; and this sort of thing has been going on in Virginia more than two years, very sad.[23]

The group slept in the open with the rain falling on them. They were so tired, the rain did not affect their slumber.

The Second Corps made camp on a hill a mile and a half west of Fairfield. John Gordon reported that his trek to Millerstown was "a most wearisome march in mud and rain."[24]

General Lee reported that the march of the fifth "continued during the day without interruption from the enemy excepting an unimportant demonstration upon our rear . . . near Fairfield. In passing through the mountains, in advance of the column, the great length of our trains exposed them to attack by the enemy's cavalry which captured a number of wagons and ambulances."[25]

Imboden, however, on the road to Williamsport, had his anxious moments. Not only was he harassed from Greencastle during the rest of his trip to Williamsport, but he received a report that the town was in possession of the enemy. However, he discounted this as rumor. Imboden writes:

Nearly the whole of the immense train reached Williamsport on the afternoon of the 5th. . . . We took possession of the town to convert it into a great hospital for the thousands of wounded we had brought from Gettysburg. I required all the families in the place to go to cooking for the sick and wounded, on pain of having their kitchens occupied for that purpose by my men. They readily complied. A large number of surgeons had accompanied the train and these at once pulled off their coats and went to work, and soon a vast amount of suffering was mitigated. The bodies of the few who died on the march were buried. All of this was necessary because the tremendous rains had raised the river more than ten feet above the fording stage of water, and we could not possibly cross then.[26]

There were two small flat ferryboats available. As soon as the walking wounded were fed and had their wounds dressed, Imboden requisitioned the boats to take them across.

John Imboden's command consisted of the 18th Virginia Cavalry; the 62nd Virginia Infantry, Mounted; Virginia Partisan Rangers; and McClanahan's Battery.

Stuart, seeking to redeem himself after his debacle on the roads to Gettysburg, became incensed at what he considered to be one of Imboden's failures. During the Union hit-and-run attacks from Greencastle to Williamsport, Jones, leading some of Pierce's command, captured ninety of Imboden's wagons, along with 645 soldiers, most of them wounded men. Stuart, in his anger, called for a court of inquiry. This was the only real criticism of Imboden, and with just over two thousand men stretched over seventeen miles, he can hardly be faulted.

Meanwhile, on this rainy, sleepy Sunday, the news of the victory at Gettysburg began reaching the large cities of the North.

George Templeton Strong was an outstanding New York lawyer, a trustee of Columbia College, a vestryman of Trinity Church, and treasurer of the Sanitary Commission which did so much for the wounded in the Civil War. He kept a diary during the Civil War, and that day he wrote:

> Tidings from Gettysburg have been arriving in fragmentary installments, but with a steady crescendo toward complete, overwhelming victory. If we can believe what we hear, Lee is smitten . . . and his invincible 'Army of Northern Virginia' shattered and destroyed. . . . There has been a great battle in which we are, on the whole, victorious.

Strong added that the news was enough to make us "thank God for most devoutly." The situation had changed so drastically in a week. Earlier, the cities and the nation had been threatened. Now it appeared that the threat was over. "This may have been one of the great decisive battles of history." Indeed it was.

Strong notes that this first Sunday in July was "a day of quiet rain." Perhaps it was typical of the tears of sorrow being shed by many over the loss of loved ones.

While the North was beginning to rejoice, George Meade sent Marsena Patrick into Gettysburg to make arrangements for the gruesome tasks of burying the dead. Patrick conferred with the Honorable David Wills.

Back in Gettysburg, Meade's problems were more complicated than Lee's. Marse Robert had but one choice. Meade had several options, and also had to wonder what Lee might do. Lee was tricky and Meade thought that he might fall back and lead him into a trap or into a battle on ground he had selected.

Lee on the west side of the battlefield had access to the shorter route to the Potomac. He also had the advantage of retreating under cover of darkness. However, the heavy rain was to wipe out part of this advantage.

Meade did not think Lee would resume the offensive, but he could not be sure, and he had been ordered to protect Washington and Baltimore. If he moved too quickly, he might endanger these cities. If he left first, he might convey the idea that he had lost. In the Civil War the notion prevailed that the vanquished left the field first.

Meade made plans to follow Lee to the east of the mountains, thus taking the longer route. He felt that the Rebels could use the mountain passes to create serious delay in follow-up.

The debate still rises whether Meade should have vigorously pursued Lee. Charles Wainwright, an artillery officer in the First Corps, feels that Meade was correct in his July 5 decisions.

> July 5, Sunday. Lee has cleared out; gone off to the westward during the night with all his army. He evidently waited yesterday to give Meade a chance to attack him; perhaps, too, in order to get his trains well started on the way. Meade was too wise to try to attack and so Lee cleared off. A number of our generals I know think that we ought to have attacked. I for one am glad that he did not. Lee had doubtless lost very heavily, but we had suffered almost as much, and our men were quite as much exhausted as his. In every respect the two armies are so well balanced that the assaulting party is sure to fail if the other has time to post itself and do anything at entrenching. This has been shown in every battle so far, unless the generalship was very bad. Here Lee had a position quite as strong or stronger. He was probably somewhat short of artillery ammunition, but not of small arm or canister. Americans of both sides are not elated by success or depressed by defeat as most people are. The Saxon bulldog blood in them would have made the rebels fight harder than ever to pay off the scores of Friday; while I could plainly see that our men thought they had had fight enough for once.
>
> On strictly scientific grounds perhaps we ought to have attacked, but taking the composition of the two armies into consideration, I feel sure that Meade was right in not doing it.[27]

Ted Gerrish of the 20th Maine of the Fifth Corps had other ideas.

On the fifth of July, the Army of the Potomac turned from the battlefield of Gettysburg, upon which they left sixteen thousand of their comrades killed and wounded, and began the pursuit of General Lee. The pursuit had been delayed too long, for it had given the rebel chieftan twenty-four hours' advantage. General Lee had left his dead unburied, and his wounded uncared for, and with his defeated army was making forced marches to endeavor to recross the Potomac River before our army could overtake him. On every hand there were indications of defeat and demoralization of his army. If ours had been a vigorous pursuit he would not have reached the Potomac, and the destiny of the rebellion would have been determined upon the plains of Maryland.[28]

The Fifteenth New Jersey went forward to probe the Confederate lines. Near the top of farmer's hill a few shots were exchanged, and descending through the woods on the other side we soon met the enemy's skirmishers. The Third Regiment and Company B of the Fifteenth were deployed, and the line not being found long enough, a momentary halt was made while a company from one of the regiments in the rear of another brigade was deployed. These men came forward very handsomely. With a cheer they ran down the hill, deploying as they came. They joined the left of our line, and the whole swept forward, driving the enemy from the woods and across the field beyond. There was considerable firing, but our casualties were not numerous. One man from the Third Regiment was killed and two were wounded. The dead man we buried on the spot. As General Torbert rode along our regiment a bullet took a button off his coat breast. We drove the enemy a full mile. Two of their number were killed, and we took six prisoners. A Georgia Lieutenant named Walker was severely wounded and fell into our hands. Dr. Hall dressed his wounds, as best he could in the haste in which we were moving. The man was then carried to the roadside and laid where he could be seen and taken up by the ambulances should they come this way.

A man and his wife who lived on a little house in the wood through which we skirmished were for a time in great jeopardy, being between lines. They ran into the house and then out, in doubt as to the safer place for them, the balls going through their frail tenement.

After the skirmish we cautiously ascended a swell of land, where we were halted until night came down upon us. Leaving a line of pickets, the lines of battle moved back to the woods and we went into camp, being in the vicinity of Fairfield, Pennsylvania, and in the left of the Gettysburg and Hagerstown Road.[29]

James Bowen also noted that the advance was sickening. The Sixth Corps moved forward amidst the unburied of July 3. It was a horrible spectacle. Everywhere the sad debris of the conflict met the eye. The wounded had all been gathered into the vast field hospitals, but the dead were still unburied. Large details from the Second Corps were at work on that sad duty by marking the resting place of each comrade with a piece of board, which had recently formed part of a cracker box, bearing the name, rank, company and regiment of the fallen hero. Great numbers of the Confederate dead still lay exposed to the elements, scores of horses were strewn around as they had fallen, weapons and equipments of every kind were scattered in every direction. Gettysburg was left behind and the regiment pushed along the Fairfield Road. In the pursuit, additional evidence of the terrible losses of the enemy constantly multiplied. "Every building was filled with Confederate wounded; in sheltered spots in the corners of fences, wherever an approach to comfort could be found, the unfortunate men had been left to the tender mercies of the victors—mercies, be it recorded, which never failed to succor and care for the misguided men as tenderly as though they had fallen in defense of the Stars and Stripes. Yet, Lee's long wagon trains had been packed to their utmost capacity with wounded, whom he was attempting to transport back to Virginia."

"The day's march was short, not more than seven or eight miles being covered. The roads were muddy and very tedious, and early in the afternoon the advance came so close upon the rebel rear that it was necessary to proceed with caution. Evening showed the enemy's rear guard strongly disposed to dispute the passage of the pursuers through the South Mountains, which had now been reached, and a halt for the night was ordered. Many had been the demonstrations of delight along the route by the loyal people, some of whom came from miles away to look upon the valiant veterans who had freed them from the presence of the hateful foe. There was everywhere the realization of a crushing defeat sustained by the invaders, their own wounded and prisoners frankly admitting for the first time that they had been worsted by the Yankees policy of leaving the defensive in Virginia and assuming the offensive on Northern soil."[30]

XII CORPS—USA

The XII Corps remained on the battlefield during the night of the fourth, and moved early the next morning in the direction of Littlestown. The men were glad when the command moved to rid themselves of the mud and stench; the latter was perceptible for miles away.

As the respective regiments marched out on the Baltimore Pike, the losses could be more fully appreciated. Some of the regiments and companies had new commanding officers. Comrades, who had been accustomed to march in the ranks and cheer the men with their smiles and jokes, were not there and the survivors were sad in spite of their efforts to be gay and cheerful. One regiment was noticed standing by the roadside, which went into the fight at least five hundred strong, but did not now exceed a hundred. The survivors looked sad and mournful, and many eyes in the moving column were filled with tears.

It was Sunday afternoon when they arrived in Littlestown; the stores and business places were closed, the streets deserted, and everything was quiet and orderly, but it was muddy, and when the brigade pickets filed into the fields through the deep grass and growing corn, they were wet from head to foot. At ten o'clock they were posted, and the reserves located on the roads leading into Littlestown. Most of the men had thrown away their woolen blankets during the recent engagement and were fortunate if they had even a rubber one. They were worn out with fatigue and excessive nervous strain, and when their duties permitted, sought rest by lying on the cold wet ground. Soon a driving storm came and continued late the next morning. The men were so fatigued they were not disturbed by the rain until little streams of water ran through their clothes. They then leaned against the trees and sat with their heads bowed on their breasts and dozed while the rain wet them to the skin. It was a terrible night and the suffering of the pickets was great.

Silas Colgrove probed what had been the Confederate defenses. He led his men into the streets of Gettysburg and found the rebels had gone. The remainder of the day was spent in the gruesome task of burying the dead of both sides, and caring for the wounded.

Some of the men in the ranks were grumbling, including Edmund Brown of the 27th Indiana. He felt history would condemn Meade for allowing Lee to slip away from Gettysburg. Brown felt that Meade's failure to continue the action was an indication that Meade had not yet reached the ranks of being a great commander. Brown and his comrades waited all day for an order to attack. It never came.[31]

I CORPS—USA

The I Corps left Gettysburg with thinned ranks. They had fought west of Gettysburg and bought precious time while other units of the army were able to assemble. Of 8,500 men carried into action on the first of July, 5,492 were listed as killed, wounded or missing. This figure is for infantry only. It does not include the I Corps Artillery. The famous Iron Brigade, the 2nd, 6th, 7th Wisconsin, 19th Indiana, and 24th Michigan were exceptionally hard hit.

During the war, Sergeant Sullivan D. Green of the 24th Michigan sent letters and articles to the Detroit *Free Press*. The tragedy of Gettysburg is told in three of his letters.

> Culp's Hill, July 2, 1863—If ever one sat down with a sad heart to write, that task is mine this morning, surrounded by the broken fragments of the Twenty-fourth which has now indeed "been all cut in pieces." Seven officers and four of them wounded are all we have with us, out the Twenty-eight and ninety-nine men out of five hundred and seventeen in yesterday's

field report, after the fiercest battle of the war. Our list of killed and wounded receives additions every few hours, from the missing who bring us names of those they saw fall. This fearful list tells in what a storm of balls they stood their ground, slowly falling back with firm and bloody front to foe, foot by foot, first to the fence then behind trees and piles of wood, and finally through the town, while a deadly fire, in flank and rear, cut through the streets. The day for us was fearful and our thoughts turn to those at home whose dear ones lie on yonder field; some in their last gory sleep, others suffering from wounds and no aid near them. Some were struck while passing through the town and most of those captured were taken there.

On Battlefield, July 4, 1863—Colonel Morrow has just come out of the city, which the enemy left during the night, but their lines still incise our first and bloodiest field. Last night the Colonel visited that scene of conflict and brought in some of the wounded who had lain there three days with no care except what the rebels bestowed, who gave them water and treated them well. They, however, stripped and robbed the bodies of the dead who still lie there so bloated as to be unrecognizable. Our wounded were full of enthusiasm, though unable to move, with limbs crushed and swollen, and with out food. They greeted the Colonel with a cheer and asked him how he was now satisfied with the Twenty-fourth.

On battlefield, Sunday, July 5, 1863—We have changed position to near the scene of the rebel's desperate and final charge. Here are evidences of the struggle—the ground trampled down; buildings riddled with shot or in black ruins; trees cut and fences splintered with grape on Pickett's charge. Details are still burying the rebel dead, and the long trenches of fresh filled earth attest the fullness of death's harvest, while lesser heaps of rocks and clumps of bushes show where a sharpshooter net his fate.

Yonder is the crest of a shallow ravine, thickly wooded the field whence came the attacking forces to defeat and death. Between yonder belts of timber a mile away is the field of the Twenty-fourth's dead. Our comrades lie there unburied on the field consecrated with their blood. Some of our boys have visited the field and the doubt that hung over the fate of the missing has been partly cleared away. That list, so full of suspense, has been diminished and the killed and wounded lists increased.[32]

Colonel Wainwright and others tell of the problem of burying the dead:

During the morning I rode out over the ground of the first day's fight. Very few of our dead were buried and some of their own even had been left lying where they fell. The bodies presented a ghastly sight, being swollen almost to the bursting of their clothes, and the faces perfectly black. Burying parties were out gathering all the dead, but the work of burying them was very ineffectually done, for twenty or more were put in a trench side by side, and covered with only a foot or two of earth. The details from the different corps for this work were very large. I hear that they report this evening near 5,000 rebel dead buried, including 1,200 around Culp's Hill. This last I do not believe, from that I saw there myself yesterday morning.[33]

Thomas Gawley says that the dead were brought in from the fields, and counted. The Confederates were placed in one row, the Union soldiers in another. At the foot of fifty or a hundred dead, a trench was dug, about three feet deep and eight feet wide. Then the bodies, blackened from exposure to the sun and elements, were placed in the trench and covered with dirt.

Civilian souvenir hunters were all over the fields, picking up relics. Many had satchels slung across their shoulders or carried bags. Many reached the battlefield by gaining permission to serve as volunteer male nurses. However, they had no intention of rendering such service. Some doctors and ministers did come for that purpose and rendered valuable help. It seems as though cannonballs were considered prize finds.[34]

II CORPS—USA

At 11:00 a.m., the II Corps disengaged from its line of battle in the Union center on Cemetery Ridge. They struck across muddy fields to the Baltimore Pike, and headed for Two Taverns and Littlestown, Pennsylvania.

Coming north, Meade had advanced using the roads as fingers of a glove. To a degree he was going after Lee in the same manner. This time the Union II and XII Corps would march together. The II Corps camped at Two Taverns until July 7. Due to a shortage of food, each man had to forage for himself. Each soldier was expected to pay for the food he obtained from the farmers and civilians.

Meanwhile, the historian of the 141st Pennsylvania describes what it was like in the front on this rainy Sunday.

Sunday, the 5th, the rain continued to fall at intervals, breaking up the roads, transforming the soft soil into a mortar bed, rendering the movements of infantry difficult and of wagon and artillery trains almost impossible. All day the regiment remains under its shelters awaiting orders to start in pursuit of the foe whose retreat toward the Potomac is now ascertained. The day is spent in removing the wounded, burying the dead and gathering the arms and accouterments with which the field was strewn. The officers and men availed themselves of the opportunity to go over the fields and carefully survey the scene of the terrible strife in which they had been engaged. On the sixth, Lieutenant Atkinson writes:—"Yesterday I went over the battlefield. I will not attempt to describe it. I dread to think of it. I went on the ground where our regiment did its hardest fighting. I there found twenty-seven of the dead of our regiment on a very small space of ground—four of my company. Our brigade of six regiments numbers less than six hundred men. We are under marching orders an liable to move at any moment." The orders were, however, countermanded, and the Regiment remained in its position until Tuesday[35]

Henry Taylor was pondering his sad mission, accomplished on July 3. A member of the 1st Minnesota told Henry he had found the body of his dead brother. Henry went to the cold, lifeless body of his brother, "secured his pocketbook, watch, diary, knife, etc., and with Wm. E. Bundy and J. S. Brown buried him at 10 o'clock a.m."

Henry inscribed on the headboard "he lay like a warrior taking his rest, with his shelter tent around him." Also chiseled into the wood were these words:

I. L. Taylor 1st Minn. Vol. Buried at 10 o'clock, a.m. on July 3, 1863 By his brother Sgt. P. H. Taylor co. "E" 1t Minn Vols[36]

V CORPS—USA

The V Corps had been heavily engaged at Little Round Top. On the hill, the 20th Maine had fought a classic battle against Longstreet's men. Strong Vincent and many of his men had given "their last full measure of devotion" to hold the strategic heights.

Captain James A. Bade, chief of the V Corps ambulances, was catching a little rest. When the Confederate artillery started to shell Cemetery Ridge on July 3, the wounded of the corps were getting hit by the missiles going over the line of battle. Thus, the hospitals had to be moved. Bade used eighty-one ambulances to move the 2,600 wounded of the V Corps. This took him two days as he moved them a mile and a half to the rear.

George Sykes, the new commander of the V Corps, contemplated the movement against Lee. His orders were to head south to Emmitsburg, and then take the Old Frederick Road through Creagarstown and Utica Post Office. Five days would be required to travel fifty-five miles and cross two mountains.

The historian of the 118th Pennsylvania writes that the soldiers shook off their wet clothing like a dog after a bath. Clothing was hung out to absorb the bright, warm rays of the sun. About 6:00 p.m., the 118th departed from the base of Little Round Top and marched southward to Marsh Creek. Camp was made about 11:00 p.m.[37]

Oliver Norton rode over the battlefield that day. He shares his impressions.

The past three have been eventful weeks and I begin to hope the back of the rebellion is broken. If the Mississippi had any special relation to the monster, it certainly is, for yesterday we received official information that the river was open. At Gettysburg I think we broke the ribs on one side. At all events we came nearer to it than we ever did before. Oh, that was a terrible fight! I rode over a great part of the ground on the left, on the 5th, and of all the carnage I ever say that was the most horrible. All over the field were scattered black and bloated corpses of men and dead horses, wrecks of caissons and gun carriages. I was galloping along the road when all at once my horse sprang to one side, and looking to see what started him, I saw the bodies of thirteen rebels lying in the mud with the pitiless rain beating on the ghastly faces. That would have been a horror at home; there it was only a glimpse of what might be seen. The rebels buried immediately, and the wounded all removed that could be, by the night of the 4th.[38]

III CORPS—USA

Back in Washington, Dan Sickles, the wounded commander of the III Corps, was making political hay. John Rusling, a staff member who had been detained in Washington during the battle, found Sickles at a private home opposite the Ebbitt House. Rusling made a call at 3:00 p.m. on the fifth, and while he was there a distinguished visitor came:

We had not been talking long, when an orderly announced his excellency the President; and immediately . . . Mr. Lincoln walked into the room, accompanied by his son, Tad. . . . He was staying out at the Soldier's Home, but having learned of General Sickle's arrival . . . rode in on horseback to call on him, with a squad of cavalry as escort. They shook hands cordially. . . . It was easy to see that they both held each other in high esteem.[39]

After the exchange of greeting, Mr. Lincoln dropped into a chair and started to question Sickles about the combat at Gettysburg, the losses and the care of the wounded. Naturally he asked Sickles first of all about his amputated leg.

Dan Sickles listened while hanging onto his cigar. Then despite his wound and weakened condition he went into great detail about the battle. Sometimes Dan winced with pain, and occasionally he asked an orderly to wet his fevered stump. But he never dropped his cigar, nor lost the point of discussion. He made sure he got his side of the story of Gettysburg to the President. No doubt it helped when Meade proposed to court martial Sickles for his actions in the Peach Orchard.

There was a pause in the conversation, and Sickles puffed on his cigar. Then he asked, "Well, Mr. President, . . . what do you think about Gettysburg? What was your opinion while we were campaigning and fighting up there?" "Oh," replied Mr. Lincoln, "I didn't think much about it. I was not much concerned about you!" "You were not?" rejoined Sickles . . . "Why, we heard that you Washington folks were a good deal excited . . ."

"Yes, I know that. And I suppose some of us were a little rattled. . . . Some of the cabinet talked of Washington being captured, and ordered a gunboat or . . ."

When Mr. Lincoln finished, everybody was silent. The situation might be compared to the solemnity after Moses came down from Mount Sinai. Lincoln was quiet also, almost as though he was praying at that moment.

After a few words about Grant and Vicksburg, Lincoln added, "I have been praying to Almighty God for Vicksburg also. I have wrestled with Him and told Him how much we need the Mississippi . . ."

Later Rusling wrote of the visit:

"Dear Friends: I am still here; but expect to leave tomorrow. Am pretty strong again; and so anxious to rejoin, that I must go.

They have had a great fight at Gettysburg. Our corps has suffered again prodigiously. Yet, thank God! It seems to have been a good fight, and will produce great results for the good cause.

A great number of my old friends have been killed or wounded. Poor General Sickles is here. He left the corps Friday morning—having been wounded on Thursday evening—and arrived here this morning. A round shot or shell struck his right leg, just below the knee, shattering it badly; and his leg was amputated just above the knee that night. Next morning they started with him for the nearest railroad, some twenty miles off. They had to carry him on a stretcher, on their shoulders, the whole distance. On the way, the Rebel cavalry was reported at a ——— farmhouse. And what do you think? This Pennsylvania patriot, not ten miles from the battlefield, within the sound of the Rebel guns, actually charged the general and his staff for what they ate and drank that night!

They reached the railroad safely, however, and then came on here. His door has been crowded all day; but only a few admitted to see him. The President called this afternoon, while I was there, and remained some time, discussing the battle, etc. He has great confidence in Sickles, and feels his loss just now very much. The general, however, is in good spirits. He thinks he will get well; and says, as soon as his leg heals, he will give the Rebs another lick. He is not a man to despond. He says the army has won a great victory, and made the most splendid flight of the war. Am reluctant to leave him, but my duty calls me to the corps. Three of his staff are with him.[40]

While Mr. Lincoln was visiting General Sickles, Herman Haupt, the great engineer who had supervised the creation of the Union supply depot at Westminster, traveled to Gettysburg. He walked part of the way, and then obtained a buggy in New Oxford. He had also supervised repair work on the railroad line from Hanover Junction to Gettysburg.

Haupt was sure that Meade was losing a golden opportunity to crush Lee. He wired General Henry Halleck in Washington stating that he feared Meade would allow Lee to slip away unmolested. He took a dim view of Meade's effort. From then on, it seems that both Halleck and Lincoln were critical of Meade and found every excuse to pressure him to move more quickly against Lee.

By late in the day, Meade was sure, based on scouting reports from John Sedgwick, that Lee was indeed gone. He then made the decision to move via Frederick and Boonsboro against Lee, catching the Confederates at the river, rather than fighting delaying rear guard tactics by the Army of Northern Virginia.[41] From the previous experience, Meade knew that caution was needed. He was well aware of Lee's flank marches. He felt that Lee had been severely punished, but he was unaware of losses in men and supplies.

VI CORPS—USA

Sedgwick's large infantry corps was sent on a probing action on the Fairfield Road. Meade needed information, and it was hoped the VI Corps would get it.

General Sedgwick,

All the information I can obtain proves withdrawal of enemy through Cashtown and Fairfield Road. Push forward your column in W. direction; find out his force; if rear guard it will be compelled to retire; if not you'll find out. Time is of great importance, as I can't give orders for a movement without explicit information from you. General Sykes** will cover your withdrawal if necessary, and General Warren, who carries this, will read it to General Sykes.[42]

Early in the afternoon, Meade sent a dispatch to General Henry Halleck in Washington.

The enemy retired under cover of the night and heavy rain in the direction of Fairfield and Cashtown. All my available cavalry are in pursuit on the enemy's left and rear. My movement will be made at once on his flanks via Middletown and South Mountain Pass. I cannot give you the details of our capture in prisoners, colors, and arms. Upwards of twenty battle flags will be turned in from one corps. I cannot delay to pick up the debris of the battlefield and request that all those arrangement may be made by the departments. My wounded, with those of the enemy in our hands, will be left at Gettysburg. After burying our own, I am compelled to employ citizens to bury the enemy's dead. My Headquarters will be tonight at Cregerstown. Communication received from General Smith, in command of 3,000 men, on the march from Carlisle towards Cashtown. Field returns last evening give me about 55,000 effectives in the ranks, exclusive of cavalry, baggage guards, ambulance attendants, etc. Every available reinforcement is required and should be sent to Frederick without delay.[43]

Although it was dated the fourth, Meade also issued a victory statement and words of gratitude to the Army of the Potomac on the first Sunday in July.

Headquarters, Army of the Potomac,

July 4, 1863

General Orders, No. 68

The commanding General, in behalf of the country, thanks the Army of the Potomac for the glorious result of the recent operations.

An enemy superior in numbers and flushed with the pride of a successful invasion, attempted to overcome and destroy this Army. Utterly baffled and defeated, he has now withdrawn from the contest. The privations and fatigue the Army has endured, and the heroic courage and gallantry it has displayed will be matters of history to be remembered.

Our task is not yet accomplished, and the Commanding General looks to the Army for greater efforts to drive from our soil every vestige of the presence of the invader.

It is right and proper that we should, on all suitable occasions, return our grateful thanks to the Almighty Disposer of events, that in the goodness of His Providence He has thought fit to give victory to the cause of the just. By command of Major-General Meade.

Official

S. Williams,

Asst. Adjt. Gen.[44]

Toward evening, communiqués from Sedgwick led Meade to believe that the Army of Northern Virginia was strongly posted in the Fairfield Pass, and that a fight could be expected. Meade therefore directed the III and V Corps to move toward Fairfield to support the VI Corps. Their mission was to assist Sedgwick or reinforce him as the situation required.

Earlier Meade had prepared a circular directing the Army of the Potomac by way of Frederick in pursuit of Lee. Although it was ready to be passed on to the corps commanders, Meade did not want to release it until he knew what was going to happen at Fairfield. But Dan Butterfield, the chief of staff, had gone ahead and issued the circular on his own authority without Meade's knowledge and permission. This caused temporary chaos and confusion. Orders were coming from both Meade and Butterfield. When Meade realized what had happened, staff officers were sent to recall the III and V Corps. Thus, the march of the Army of the Potomac from Gettysburg started on an order released prematurely by the chief of staff.

The circular detailing the Union movement gave these directives:

The following movements of troops are ordered: The 1st, 6th and 3rd Corps by Emmitsburg direct road to Mechanicsburg, Lewistown, Hamburgh, to Middletown.

The 5th and 11th Corps by the left hand Taneytown road through Emmitsburg, Cregerstown, Utica, High Knob Pass to Middletown.

The 12th and 2nd Corps via Taneytown, Middleburg, and Woodsborough, through Frederick, to Middletown.

The trains will move with their corps, those at Westminster crossing to Middletown via Frederick. The Artillery Reserve follow via Taneytown and Middleburg. Headquarters will be at Cregerstown tonight. The army will assemble at Middletown p.m. of the 7th inst.

Headquarters train will move at once. All trains not filled with ammunition and supplies will be sent to Frederick. The Commissary and Quartermaster depots and supplies at Westminster will be transferred to Frederick.

The Commandant of the Cavalry Corps will detail a regiment to report to the Provost Marshall General, for the temporary duty of driving up all stragglers, and collecting all captured property, arms, ammunition, etc., on the recent battlefield.

The Medical Director will establish a General Hospital at Gettysburg for the wounded that cannot be moved with the army.

For the movement, and until the concentration at Middletown, General Sedgwick will, without relinquishing command of his Corps, assume command and direct the movements of the Corps forming the left, 12th and 2nd.

General Howard will, without relinquishing the command of his Corps, assume command and direct the movement of the Corps forming the center, 5th and 11th.

Staff officers will be sent to report at Headquarters each night on all marches.

The Battalion of Regular Engineers and other Troops at Westminster will proceed to Middletown via Frederick.

By Command of Major-General Meade

(Sd.) S. Williams

Asst. Adjt. Gen.[45]

As a result of the actions near Fairfield all troop movements were suspended.

During a lull in these operations General Meade took advantage of the opportunity, thus, offered to again write to Mrs. Meade.

Headquarters Army of the Potomac

Gettysburg, Pa. July 5, 1863

I hardly know when I last wrote to you, so many and such stirring events have occurred. I think I have written since the battle, but am not sure. It was a grand battle, and is in my judgment a most decided victory, though I did not annihilate or bag the Confederate Army. This morning they retired in great haste into the mountains, leaving their dead unburied and their wounded on the field. They awaited one day. expecting that, flushed with success, I would attack them when they would play their old game of shooting us from behind breastworks—a game we played this time to their entire satisfaction. The men behaved splendidly; I really think they are becoming soldiers.

They endured long marches, short rations, and stood one of the most terrific cannonadings I ever witnessed. Baldy was shot again, and I fear will not get over it. Two horses that George rode were killed, his own and the black mare. I had no time to think of either George or myself, for at one time things looked a little blue; but I managed to get up reinforcements in time to save the day. The army is in the highest spirits, and of course I am a great man.[46]

Toward evening, Harry Kieffer, a drummer boy with the 150th Pennsylvania, walked with a companion across the breastworks of the I Corps and the stone fences to take a look at the battlefield. All the men were talking about the battle. Some were discussing their narrow escapes as they showed holes in their hats or sleeves. Some showed crushed canteens. Many were making coffee and some were trying to sleep.

All over the place were rude headboards with the name and the regiment of the man who had fallen. Some of the trees had been shot almost in two. And then Kieffer saw some dead yet unburied, holding onto their guns or paper, perhaps the last letter from home.

Tracks of blood, even to the forest's depths,

And scattered arms, and lifeless warriors,

Whose lard lineaments,

Death's self could change not,

Marked the dreadful path

Of the outsallying visitors.[47]

The mud deadened the sound of the horses, marching feet, and rumbling wagons this "Rainy Sunday in July." However, the roads were full of marching men, wagons, and the implements of war. The Army of Northern Virginia stretched from Fairfield to the western base of the mountain on the Waynesboro Road.

The Union VI Corps had advanced to Fairfield. The I and III Corps were still at Gettysburg, in support of the VI. The II and XII Corps had begun marching on the Baltimore Pike and were at Two Taverns and Littlestown. The V and XI Corps were just south of Gettysburg. John Buford was at Frederick, and Kilpatrick at Smithsburg, moving toward Boonsboro.

At 10:00 p.m., an extra of *The New York Tribune* hit the newsstands. It carried glad tidings. "Lee retreating toward Williamsport. Some dispatches say that Lee has been utterly routed and disorganized. . . . Acres of cars laden with Confederate prisoners block railroads. General French has destroyed Confederate pontoon bridge at Williamsport."[48]

CIVILIANS

During the bicentennial, an old story about Smithsburg resurfaced. Alice Collingsworth was fourteen years old in July '63. She relates that soldiers of both sides were treated for wounds in Smithsburg. Injured from blue and gray were patients in the Bell home. The family played it safe by keeping flags from both the North and South close by. According to young Alice, Custer ate dinner in the home of a Mr. Webber. She was impressed with the general's long blonde hair and deep blue eyes.[49]

Miss Collingsworth and others said that General Lee stopped in Smithsburg. This was hardly Robert E. Lee, but the cavalry officer, Fitzhugh Lee. Two hours after the Confederate cavalry arrived, a daughter was born to Dr. and Mrs. Riddlemoser. Fitz Lee was staying in the home, so the new baby was named Effie Lee.

Meanwhile in New York, the *Tribune* was setting the print for Monday's headlines.

> Great Victory. The Rebel Army Totally defeated. Its remains driven into the mountains it is there surrounded and hemmed in. Its retreat across the Potomac cut off.[50]

BUFORD'S CAVALRY—USA

John Buford's entire division reached Frederick having ridden from Westminster. Their exact route is difficult to determine. The day was spent in drawing supplies, repairing horseshoes, etc.

The 8th Illinois, the regiment that fired the opening shots at Gettysburg, camped about a mile west of Frederick on the road to Middletown. Soon after their arrival, they had a visitor. They had seen him around the camps prior to Gettysburg. He was "nosy, always asking too many questions." The visitor claimed his name was Richardson, and a resident of Baltimore. He stated that he was interested in the religious welfare of the troops and handed out tracts. However, Provost Marshal Mix was very suspicious and arrested Richardson. A personal search revealed passes from both Union and Confederate generals. He said the passes were on his person because he had three sons in Confederate service, and had gone to see them.

Richardson was taken to Buford, who was convinced they had indeed caught a major spy. The General said, "Hang him." The spy was given a few moments to prepare his soul for eternity. He tried to escape. Quickly a rope was placed around his neck, thrown over a tree limb, and he was hanged by three soldiers. His body was left hanging for several days, perhaps as an example.[51]

Devin's brigade of the division did not arrive in Frederick until 6:00 p.m. They had ridden for twelve hours from Uniontown to Middleburg, Woodsboro and thence to Frederick.

—3—
Armies on the Move
Monday, July 6, 1863

From the mountain, and from positions near Waynesboro, Pennsylvania, the Army of Northern Virginia continued their movements toward the Potomac River. John Imboden sought to ease the suffering of the wagon train of misery. He placed the wounded in the public buildings and churches in Williamsport, including the Roman Catholic Church.

Meanwhile, to the northeast, John Sedgwick and the Union VI Corps made a reconnaissance in force toward Fairfield. At 8:30, "Uncle John," as he was affectionately called by his men, sent a dispatch to Meade saying he felt the Confederate position in the mountain was very strong and "I do not like to dash my corps against it."[1] Sedgwick was also concerned about protection for his right flank. The Army of the Potomac knew how the Confederates fought from fixed positions, such as the heights above Burnside Bridge at Sharpsburg, and at Marye's Heights at Fredericksburg. There was no way Sedgwick could flank the Rebel position. His only approach was a frontal assault, and this meant the Confederates had the advantage.

Half an hour later, a message came from General Meade saying that Gregg's Union cavalry had ridden westward, passing through Cashtown and Caledonia. They found no sign of any Southern soldiers. Thus, Sedgwick's flank was clear. Meade also stated he did not think Lee would fight unless attacked. Meade believed he wanted to reach the Potomac River as quickly as possible.

VI CORPS—USA

Sedgwick moved cautiously. The morning was very foggy. The brigade of Thomas Neill moved toward the mountain gap. The fog and the terrain slowed the advance. On the basis of the number of Confederate campfires, noted the previous evening, it was thought the gap was strongly fortified. Sedgwick ordered a halt and awaited orders. He thought it would take a long time and great effort to dislodge Lee from the pass. Upon

40

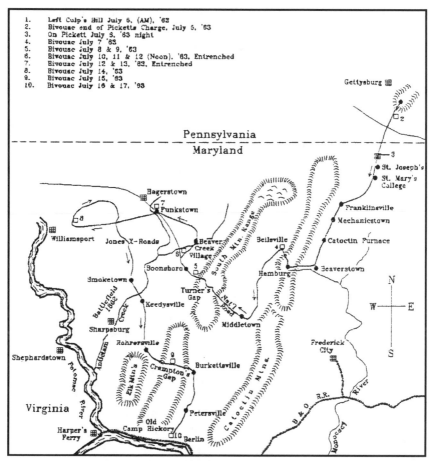

1. Left Culp's Hill July 5, (AM), '63
2. Bivouac end of Pickett's Charge, July 5, '63
3. On Pickett July 5, '63 night
4. Bivouac July 7 '63
5. Bivouac July 8 & 9, '63
6. Bivouac July 10, 11 & 12 (Noon), '63, Entrenched
7. Bivouac July 12 & 13, '63, Entrenched
8. Bivouac July 14, '63
9. Bivouac July 15, '63
10. Bivouac July 16 & 17, '63

Route of the Iron Brigade
Steps of the I and VI Corps

History of the Twenty-fourth Michigan, p. 898

receipt of the information from Sedgwick, Meade ordered the army to con-
centrate west of Frederick at Middletown, Maryland. The Army of the
Potomac would then be near South Mountain, and between R. E. Lee and
Washington, D.C. Neill's brigade and some cavalry were to remain in
Fairfield, while the rest of the VI Corps was to proceed to Emmitsburg.[2]

John Sedgwick was also acting as commander of the right wing of
the Army of the Potomac. The command included his own corps, as well
as the I and the XII.

After probing Lee's rear guard, the VI Corps, with the exception of
one brigade, proceeded to Emmitsburg. There they halted for five hours.
The spirits of the 37th Massachusetts were brightened as they received a
full sack of mail. Most of the troops also got their first rations in thirty-six

hours. The food didn't last long. After all, marching in the rain makes one hungry. Another eighteen hours would pass before they ate again.[3]

It was time to hit the road again. Nelson Hutchinson of the 37th could still feel the experience twenty years later as night fell.

Alfred Roe was a member of the VI Corps in the advance on the foggy Monday, "Our route was on the Fairfield Road in the direction of Hagerstown. . . . The Confederates retreated through South Mountain, whose narrow pass is a short distance beyond Fairfield. Here they planted artillery so that their ranks might be protected as they filed through. General Sedgwick pronounced the position too strong for assault."[4]

Nelson Hutchinson, also a member of the VI Corps, noted that along the way to Fairfield, "Everywhere lay debris of war, thousands of men and horses swollen beyond recognition. . . . The stench was unbearable. . . . Every farmhouse was filled to overflowing with the dead and wounded of Lee's army."[5]

Toward evening, most of the VI Corps was back in Fairfield. The column was halted for food and rest. Then about 10:00 p.m., they marched to Emmitsburg.

I CORPS—USA

The I Corps took the roads from Gettysburg in reverse of the march to the fields of Pennsylvania. They headed south in the midst of a driving rain. Several hours later, they arrived in Emmitsburg, eleven miles away. They marched past their June 30 bivouac at Marsh Creek, and the location of the headquarters of General John Reynolds. There was elation, because this time they had forced Lee to retire from the battlefield. However, there was sadness over the loss of so many comrades.

About 2:00 p.m., Rufus Dawes wrote to his family:

> This has been a terrible ordeal. Our loss is 30 killed outright, 116 wounded . . . and 25 missing, all from 340 men taken into battle. . . . The experience of the past few days seem more like a horrible dream than reality. May God save me and my men from any more such anguish.[6]

Although Charles Wainwright rode in the rain, he never felt dirtier in his life. For six days he did not even have a clean handkerchief. He stopped and washed it in a stream. He also washed his feet.

Wainwright and most of his companions were glad to be out of Pennsylvania. They were met in Emmitsburg by the Sisters of Charity. The nuns came with several large wagons of food. Some of the contents were shared with the troops. The rest was taken to Gettysburg for the wounded. Many surgeons of the I Corps were left at Gettysburg to treat the wounded.[7]

Henry Kieffer, the drummer boy of the 150th Pennsylvania, was close to tears. He recalled boiling meat in Emmitsburg with his friends, Sam and Joe Ruhl, and Jimmy Lucas. They were members of the regimental color guard. Twenty-four hours later, two of them were dead, numbered along the fallen on McPherson's Ridge.[8]

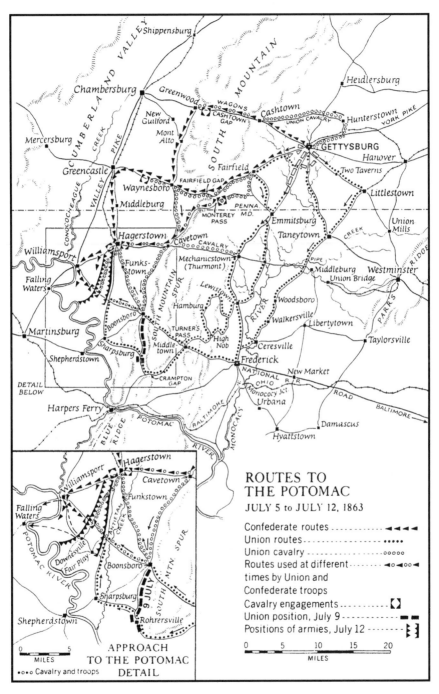

Shippensburg

CUMBERLAND VALLEY

Chambersburg
Greenwood
WAGONS
CASHTOWN GAP
Cashtown
UNION CAVALRY
Hunterstown
YORK PIKE

Mercersburg

New Guilford
Mont Alto

SOUTH MOUNTAIN

Heidlersburg

GETTYSBURG
Hanover

Greencastle
Fairfield
FAIRFIELD GAP

Two Taverns

Littlestown

Waynesboro

CREEK

Middleburg
MONTEREY PASS
PENNA. MD.

Union Mills

CONOCHEAGUE CREEK

VALLEY PIKE

Hagerstown
Cavetown
CAVALRY

Emmitsburg
Taneytown

PARRS RIDGE

Williamsport

Funks-town

Mechanicstown (Thurmont)

PIPE CREEK
Middleburg
Union Bridge
Westminster

Falling Waters

SOUTH MOUNTAIN SPUR

Lewistown

Woodsboro

Hamburg

Walkersville
Libertytown

Martinsburg

Boonsboro

TURNER'S PASS
High Nob

RIVER

Ceresville

Taylorsville

Sharpsburg
Middletown

Shepherdstown

Frederick

New Market

DETAIL BELOW

CRAMPTON GAP

NATIONAL
OHIO R.R.
Monocacy Jct.
Urbana

ROAD
BALTIMORE

Harpers Ferry

BLUE RIDGE
POTOMAC

BALTIMORE

MONOCACY RIVER

Damascus

Hyattstown

Hagerstown
Cavetown

Williamsport

Funkstown

Falling Waters

ANTIETAM CREEK

SOUTH MTN. SPUR

Downsville
Fair Play

Boonsboro

POTOMAC RIVER

Sharpsburg

9 JULY

Shepherdstown

Rohrersville

0   5
MILES
•o•o Cavalry and troops

APPROACH
TO THE POTOMAC
DETAIL

ROUTES TO
THE POTOMAC
JULY 5 to JULY 12, 1863

Confederate routes .... ◄◄◄
Union routes .... •••••
Union cavalry .... ooooo
Routes used at different ..... ◄o◄oo◄
times by Union and
Confederate troops
Cavalry engagements .... 【】
Union position, July 9 .... ■ ■
Positions of armies, July 12 .... 〉 〈

0   5   10   15   20
MILES

Meade Advances in the Valley of the Antietam

Edwin B. Coddington, *The Gettysburg Campaign*,
Charles Scribner's, 1968, p. 548

Marsena Patrick had to go into Gettysburg prior to heading south to shod two of his horses. The rocks at Gettysburg had been rough on their feet. Patrick also had a visitor. General Isaac Trimble, CSA, wanted to know if he could be brought from the field hospital to Gettysburg as he lost his leg in Pickett's charge. He also wished his family to come from Baltimore and take him home. Meade and Trimble had been old friends, so Patrick granted the request. The two had a pleasant half an hour interview.[9]

Patrick was appalled at the condition of the battlefield. Many of the men of the I Corps had not been buried. . . . Their bodies presented a most hideous spectacle.[10]

II CORPS—USA

The II Corps, at least portions of it, left the field on Sunday. Frank Sawyer and the 8th Ohio had gone to Two Taverns east of Gettysburg. On Monday, they visited some of the farms. They were surprised to find themselves unwelcome. A plump Dutch woman refused to permit the soldiers into her kitchen. She said they were too "ornery." She wanted a dollar for a gallon of milk, and a half of a dollar for a cruet of vinegar.[11]

Men of the II and XII Corps who followed were amazed at the high prices charged by the citizens. On the roads to Gettysburg, the people were anxious for their safety. Now that the Confederate threat no longer existed, many sought to get the highest possible price from the tired and hungry Union soldiers. One soldier was angry and threatened to burn a Dutch barn.[12]

They found a warmer reception in Maryland. Once across the state line, they found many with wagons of milk and hands outstretched with goodies. In Taneytown, two ladies worked around the clock baking fresh bread for "The Saviors of the Republic."

From camp near Two Taverns, Henry Taylor, of the First Minnesota, wrote to his parents about the death of his brother Isaac. He told them the shell took off part of his head. The letter said:

> . . . I have Isaac's things and will send most of them home but I shall keep his watch with your permission. He wished Father to have his diary. . . .

> Isaac has not fallen in vain. What though one of your six sons has fallen on the altar of our country, 'tis a glorious death; better die free than live as slaves. Pleas (his spelling) make no arrangements for his funeral until you hear from me again. . . . I cannot express to you my sorrow at his loss. I feel as though I was all alone.

> Yours and my country's

> Henry[13]

Prior to departing from Gettysburg, Henry had gone to Isaac's grave and placed stones around it.[14]

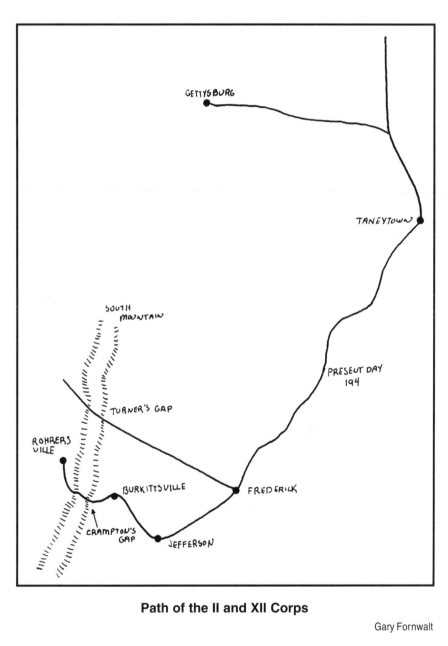

Path of the II and XII Corps

Gary Fornwalt

III CORPS—USA

Charlie Bardeen, another of the "little drummer" boys, disliked marching in the rain. However, he took solace in the fact, "We marched back to Virginia as victors." The historian of the 17th Maine notes the regiment marched seventeen miles on a "damp, rainy, and disagreeable day."[15] The country was deluged by rain. Their destination was Mechanicstown, modern day Thurmont.

Samuel Toombs of the 13th New Jersey writes:

The morning of the 6th of July was rainy and disagreeable. Orders had been received to move at daylight, and soon the whole column was in motion. Those who may imagine that the march of an army is simply a parade of troops on a large scale; that bands of music with a drum major, in gaudy uniform, precedes each regiment or brigade; that the soldiers carry their muskets to a "shoulder arms," or "right shoulder shift," as they have witnessed militia regiments on parade at home, that each regiment marches company front, every man keeping perfect step, astonished to know that their imaginations are at fault. The first announcement of marching orders is communicated by the Sergeant-Major to the Orderly-Sergeants of the different companies, who notify the men. Tents are at once struck, and rolled up with rubber or woolen blankets into a long roll. Equipments, haversacks and canteens are all placed together, and until the assembly call is beat, the men lounge around smoking, playing cards, or indulging in some innocent pastime. At the sound of the drum equipments are donned, the men stand up in front of the stacks of muskets to the position of "Attention," and at the command "Take Arms!" is next given, each piece being raised to the right side, and then at the command "Right Face" the column forms in four ranks—four men abreast—when (sometimes the command "Forward" is given, frequently not) the regiment moves out to the road, taking its assigned position in line for the day, either first, second, third, or last, as may be. So far the strict military form has been observed, but as soon as the column starts upon the road, guns are slung across the shoulder and carried muzzle down, some are at a "right shoulder shift," others carried across the left shoulder, while some of the men find relief by loosening the strap of the gun and throwing it across their bodies diagonally to the roll composed of a piece of tent and a blanket, which is carried by being on the arm of the opposite side. Some of the men have knapsacks strapped to their backs, but by far the greater number are without that bulky and superserviceable structure.

Thus the appearance of a column of troops on the march is far from imposing, as compared with a finely uniformed and gaily equipped body of militia on parade, and is in direct contrast to the preconceived ideas of those who have never witnessed a sight of this kind. Each regiment changes position in line daily, and each brigade of a division is also assigned a new place in the line on every march, so that during a campaign all have an equal chance

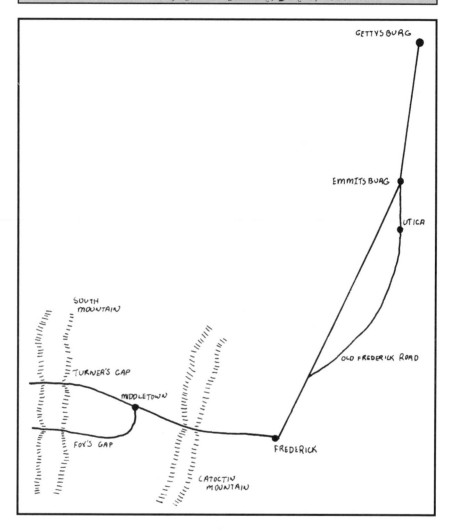

Route of the III and V Corps

Gary Fornwalt

to share in the honors attached to "the right of the line." A division generally marches in unbroken column. The infantry always marches ahead followed by the artillery, after which comes the ambulance corps, and lastly the wagon train. The troops on the right of the line have the best time of it, particularly on a long march, such as the one I am about to describe proved to be. By the time the head of the column had marched four or five miles, and turned into a field on the road, stacked arms, and were enjoying a brief rest, the roads were little better than ditches. "The shallow streams near the roads had swollen into considerable streams."[16]

THE XII CORPS—USA

Slocum's Corps left the northern end of the fishhook line on Cemetery Ridge, and headed east to Littlestown. Some of the officers went into the village seeking food. They were starved. A lady invited them to partake of some freshly baked pies. They feasted on cherry and berry pies, along with biscuits and milk. The food was delicious. They thought they were being fed in gratitude. However, one officer asked, "Is there any cost?" The lady replied promptly, "Yes, seventy-five cents." The officers paid, but were angry. They had risked life and limb, and now they were being charged for food.[17]

The historian of the 13th New Jersey describes marching from Gettysburg:

> Troops in the rear were rushing on to close up the wide gaps between the several commands. Generals and Colonels, the innocent cause of all this confusion in the rear, were being roundly abused for their "heartlessness," but still the men move along, grumbling, swearing and mad. The last regiment finally enters the field just in time to see the head of the column moving out, and the men at once throw themselves on the ground to obtain a little rest at all events. This was the way we proceeded on that march of thirty-two miles from Littlestown, Pa., to Frederick City, Md., on the 6th of July, 1863. There was incessant straggling. The rain came down in torrents during the day, but the line of march was over good turnpike road most of the time, so that no delay was occasioned, General Patrick had charge of the Provost Guard, which brought up the rear of the army, and his cavalry were kept constantly busy scouring the woods for stragglers. It was about eight o'clock at night when we neared Frederick City, and though fatigued by the long and rapid marching, every man was infused with new life as the brigade band struck up a lively air when we entered the grounds selected for our resting place.[18]

V CORPS—USA

As the V Corps began to depart from Little Round Top, Joshua Chamberlain was glad to be leaving. On Saturday, the "Glorious Fourth," he had taken some of his men down the rocky crags of Round Top. The enemy was gone. There were just the dead and wounded, men and horses. In one small field, Chamberlain found over 500 dead, blue and gray together on the bivouac of the dead.

Returning to Round Top, the 20th Maine began burying their dead. Each grave was marked with a headboard made from ammunition boxes. The soldier's name was carved into the wood. Chamberlain instructed his men to dig shallow graves for the Confederate dead. They were buried on the slopes, no marker, just young men "known but to God."

Chamberlain also visited some of the hospitals. His bother John helped to assist a wounded Confederate to higher ground to escape a rising stream. The Southern soldier said, "Never mind, we are not long for this world."[19]

On the rainy Sunday, the troops "left the hog wallows" of the battle-field. They reached Marsh Creek south of Gettysburg. Chamberlain and the others were not surprised. It rained heavily after Fredericksburg, and Chancellorsville. Now it was raining again. It was thought the heavy can-nonading disturbed the atmosphere and created the deluge.

At Marsh Creek, the men of the 20th drove their bayonets in the ground and used their weapons as poles for shelter halves. The method was not standard operating procedure, but it was quick, and kept the rifle barrels dry.[20]

FIRST CORPS—CSA

In his official report for the Gettysburg Campaign, James Longstreet notes that the First Corps followed that of A. P. Hill on the night of July 4. However, "Our march was much impeded by heavy rains and excessively bad roads."[21] The First Corps reached the top of the mountain early on the evening of July 5.

This morning, it was the First Corps' turn to lead the march of the Army of Northern Virginia to the Potomac. The exhausted men and ani-mals were in no condition for rapid movement. The First Corps reached Hagerstown about 5:00 p.m. The column, which had come through Water-loo, moved to a point two miles south of Hagerstown on the Sharpsburg Pike. Kemper's Brigade marched through the darkness, reaching Williamsport at 2:00 a.m. on the seventh.

After two hours of marching there was a brief halt. Generals Lee, Longstreet, Hill, and Wilcox met for a conference. Arthur Fremantle also saw the wounded John Bell Hood riding in carriage. The doctors were doubt-ful they could save his arm. Fremantle saw Wade Hampton, one of Jeb Stuart's lieutenants who had been shot in the hip and had received saber cuts. Somewhere along the route, Lee conferred with James Longstreet and said, "I thought my men were invincible."

Nearing Hagerstown, there was firing. The cavalry was engaged. Some of the wounded who had kept their weapons with them, jumped out of the wagons and began going to the rear. A well-dressed Union officer, smok-ing a cigar, was among them. He presented a contrast to the ragged es-cort. Many of the Confederates had not washed or shaved for a long time.

About 7:00 p.m., Lee, Longstreet, and the First Corps marched through Hagerstown. There were several dead horses, and a few dead men in the streets. Longstreet proceeded approximately one mile south of Hagerstown on the road to Williamsport, and halted for the night.

With the dawn of the following day, the best defensive positions were chosen and the First Corps remained in place until July 10.[22]

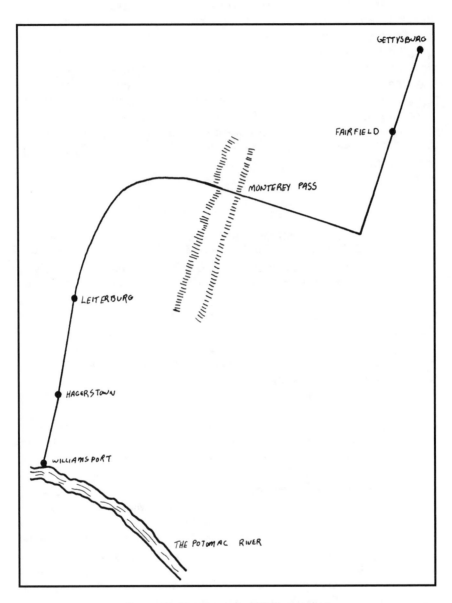

From Gettysburg to Williamsport
Route of the Army of Northern Virginia

Gary Fornwalt

There were other problems. The First Corps had barely begun to make camp when several cavalrymen, riding at top speed, came galloping into the bivouac area yelling that the entire Union cavalry was behind them. Weary Confederate infantrymen hastily grabbed their weapons and prepared to defend their camps. When the enemy arrived, it was a carriage load of lady refugees, making a lot of noise.[23]

George Pickett was lost in thought. His spirits were as gloomy as the weather. His division was gone, shot to pieces in the charge across the Emmitsburg Pike. Now the survivors of his command were entrusted with guarding the Union prisoners of war. Pickett despised the task and thought the chore was degrading. Pickett never forgave Robert E. Lee for ordering his division to charge Cemetery Ridge. The South, and later the North, regarded Lee with reverence, but to Pickett, Lee was "that old man."

Trying to escape reality, Pickett found time to write to his beloved:

It would be impossible, my darling, to describe to you even the half of the horrors and hardships of these last days, from the first night's long march to the present hour; not only for ourselves but for the prisoners whom, with shattered hopes and heartbreak we, the little remnant of my division, have been assigned to guard. "One prisoner is too many for us, who haven't a crust to go around among themselves," as Old Jack said.

Oh, the pity of it, guarding these prisoners through their country, depleted and suffering mentally and physically as we are, and being forced to march forward with a speed beyond their own and our endurance. It may be some consolation to both that we suffer alike from fatigue, hunger, exhaustion and wet, for the excessive rains which set in on the fourth have continued unabated.

The long wagon-like trains, the artillery, the assortment of vehicles of all kinds impressed from the farmers and loaded to their utmost capacity with our wounded and, anon, room made for the crowding in of yet another, falling from illness or exhaustion all along our way, have added their quota to the discomforts of the march. Our commissariat, too, has been as wretched here in this land of plenty as it was in the barren, war-ridden land we left behind. Our banquets, we, the guard of honor, and our guests, the prisoners, have shared like-and-like, and none was ever more enjoyed by either than the flour made into paste and baked on the stones, in front of the fire and the good Pennsylvania beef roasted on the end of a stick.

The prisoners have been far more cheerful than we have been, for they have not only had strong hope of being retaken by their own arms within a few days but their army has gained a great victory, and though dearly bought, it has, I fear, decided the fate of our new-born nation. The cannonading on the second morning, the shells form which we could clearly see bursting somewhere in the vicinity of the Monterey House and which we learned were from Kilpatrick's artillery, endeavoring to cut off our trains and prevent our retreat, gave the prisoners double assurance of release. Their hope of rescue being deferred at Monterey Springs, I instructed my inspector-general to parole the officers and give them safeguard to return, binding them to render themselves prisoners of war at Richmond if they were not duly recognized by their government. Unfortunately, I was not permitted to release them at this point and they were required to march with the rest of the prisoners.

Late in the evening after another trying day's march we passed Waynesboro and, with a rest of only an hour or so, marched all night. At nine o'clock the following morning we reached Hagerstown but hurried on through to Williamsport. All along the road from Hagerstown to Williamsport were gruesome evidences of Kilpatrick's dash into Hagerstown—here a dead cavalryman, there a broken caisson, a dead horse. I ought not to let your beautiful eyes see through mine all these horrors, but some day, my darling, some day we'll strew roses and violets and lilies over them all, even over the memories of them. We'll listen to the resurrection that hope and faith and love voice in al the songs of nature. It will not be long, darling, for today the official news of the surrender of Vicksburg reached us. The tidings brought cheers from the prisoners and increased the sullen gloom of their guard.

I am directed to turn the prisoners over to General Imboden's command, who is to escort them to Stanton. Their final destination will, I suppose, be the old nine-room brick warehouse on Carey Street in Richmond, "Libby & Sons—Chandlers and Grocers"—a sign which I remember as a boy and associate with "Cat" and "Traunt" and other boyish games. Always I shall like to remember it as a place to play, and not think of it as a living tomb. There will not, I fear, be many of my fellow suffers of the last days who enter these awesome walls who will ever come forth alive.

The Potomac was so swollen by the rains which began on the fourth and still continue, that it was impossible to cross it at any of the neighboring fords. A rope ferry, the only means of crossing, made it slow and tedious, and every minute's delay, my darling, seems centuries when I am on my way to you—to you.

Jackerie has waited so long for my postscript that he has gone to sleep and I have now not time to write it, but you will know that the most important thing is in the p.s. and this is love,—the love of

Your adoring

Soldier[24]

On the march, soldiers recall weather and the effort to obtain food. Edward Alexander, the officer in charge of the artillery bombardment prior to Pickett's charge, stopped at a small country store on the eastern slope of the pass and found some food. Then nearing the crest, he found an inn with lights on. He couldn't believe it was open for business as usual, with thousands of troops marching by. Stopping for some food, Alexander departed, leaving his hat behind. When he went back to get it, the hat was gone, thus, Alexander had to travel the remaining twelve hours in the rain without his headgear. Alexander lamented that the trip from near Fairfield to the Potomac required thirty-one hours of wet, muddy, fatiguing travel.[25]

SECOND CORPS—CSA

Ewell's corps "started at an early hour, continuing" the march to the Potomac. There was a heavy mist in the morning. The column moved slowly by Monterey Springs and Waterloo, and thence to Waynesboro. Ewell sent Jed Hotchkiss to Lee's headquarters at Waterloo. General Lee had good news, there was not as much loss as had been originally thought in the wagon train. Jed was given orders about the route of march, and was instructed to tell Ewell, "If these people (Yankees) keep coming on, turn back and thresh them soundly." Ewell replied, "By the blessing of Providence, I will do it."[26] Jed notes that Longstreet and Hill went to Hagerstown, while Stuart had a fight with the Yankee cavalry there. The Second Corps was able to secure some supplies in Waynesboro.

Squire Miller's Inn, Fairfield, Pennsylvania

Troops from the division of Robert Rodes replaced Early's men as skirmishers. Early, assuming the position of corps rear guard, passed through Monterey Springs, crossed the mountain, and moved to Waynesboro where he camped for the night.[27]

The falling rain added to the misery of the Stonewall Brigade as they tramped back to the Potomac. Three-fourth's of the 4th Virginia vanished at Gettysburg. On Culp's Hill, the 4th Virginia had 18 men killed, 50 wounded and 69 captured. This was the heaviest loss in the brigade. Even the prized regimental colors flag was grabbed by the 14th Connecticut. Only three members of 21st from the "Liberty Hall Volunteers" emerged unscathed. Just sixty-six men were present for the long, sad trek back to Virginia. The falling rain made the survivors feel like crying.[28]

While the troops plodded along in the mud, John Imboden was busy transporting the wounded across the swollen Potomac. The flat, ferryboats carried about thirty men at a time. It took almost fifteen minutes to cross the Potomac, unload, get food and ammunition, and recross. Thus, at least thirty minutes were required for each trip. This meant that with 10,000 men to transport to the Virginia shore, forty hours, with optimal conditions, would be required.[29]

About 6:00 a.m., Stuart in the vicinity of Smithsburg received word from Leitersburg concerning the location of the rest of the army. He was also satisfied that all of Kilpatrick's command had gone toward Boonsboro. Brigadier General Grumble Jones arrived. Surviving a narrow escape during the action at Monterey Gap and listed as captured, he made it to Williamsport. From the river, he had ridden back to report to Stuart. He also informed his commander of the arrival of Imboden's wagon train on the banks of the river.

Ferrying Troops Across the Swollen Potomac

Frank Leslie's *Illustrated*, August 1863

From the Smithsburg area, Stuart began moving. Jones was ordered to proceed to Boonsboro and thence to Funkstown "which held the eastern front to Hagerstown."

Chambliss was ordered by Stuart in Cavetown, to ride from Leitersburg directly to Hagerstown. Then he rode with Albert Jenkins' Brigade to Chewsville. In that village, Stuart received news that a large force of Union cavalry was approaching Hagerstown from Boonsboro. Jenkins was ordered forward and found the city occupied. He attempted to make a flank attack from the Chewsville-Smithsburg Road. Iverson's small brigade of Confederate infantry was at the north edge of town. Some of Stuart's men came under friendly fire. Jeb was sure the object of the Union attack was directed against Williamsport where "our wagon trains were congested in a narrow space at the foot of a hill."[30] The commanding general therefore "urged on all sides the most vigorous attack to save our trains at Williamsport." Stuart's force was smaller, "but by a bold front and determined attack. . . . I hoped to raise the siege of Williamsport."[31]

At the time, the land between Hagerstown and Williamsport was open, "almost entirely cleared, but intersected by innumerable fences and ditches." Skirmishers fought from street to street."[32]

KILPATRICK'S CAVALRY—USA

The Union troopers were astride the National Pike west of Boonsboro. Soon Buford and Kilpatrick were giving orders. Lee must be pressed, and, if possible, the Confederate wagons captured or destroyed. Soon the tired horsemen were back in the saddle. They rode into Funkstown and admired "the flagstone pavements lined with silver poplar trees." The residents were curious and wondered what was happening. They remained in their saddles and conversed briefly with the citizens. They were offered food and water, until it was time to move on.

Soon after crossing the Antietam Creek, the Union troopers encountered the pickets of the 9th Virginia Cavalry. The Confederates were protecting Hagerstown's road network. A strong Confederate force was also posted on the high ground at Key-Mar College.[33]

At noon, Kilpatrick sent a squadron on the 18th Pennsylvania Cavalry into Hagerstown. A scout led the way. Riding at the head of the column was Lieutenant Colonel William Brinton and Captains William Lindsay and Ulric Dahlgren. Entering Baltimore Street, they encountered Confederate pickets. The firing brought reinforcements from the town square. These were the men from the rest of the regiment. Some of the lads from the 13th Virginia Cavalry were eating their first hot meal in days at the Washington House. When the firing commenced, they laid aside their napkins and ran to their horses. Elements of the 10th Virginia also rushed to the fray.

At the intersection of Baltimore and South Potomac Streets, Kilpatrick's men and the 9th Virginia became heavily engaged.

A squad of the 18th Pennsylvania, led by Captains Lindsay and Dahlgren, separated from the main column and raced down South Potomac Street chasing five rebels. One of the Confederates turned and fired, killing Captain Lindsay. Dahlgren wielded his sword and split the rebel's head open.[34]

The rebels fired from the cover of alleys and houses. Heavy fighting occurred in front of St. John's Lutheran Church and in the city square. There was charge and countercharge.[35]

Ulric Dahlgren had gone for reinforcements and returned with twenty troopers from the 18th Pennsylvania. The men dismounted and began advancing, ten troopers on either side of the street. At the Market House they were met with flanking fire. Dahlgren, still mounted, was an easy target. The young captain felt a stinging sensation, but gave it little thought. However, his boot had been pierced and his foot shattered. He continued toward the Hagerstown Square, but became dizzy and fell from the saddle. His limp body was placed in an ambulance and taken to Boonsboro.[36]

After Captain Dahlgren had fallen, the 18th Pennsylvania and 7th West Virginia advanced again on Potomac Street. They were unaware that Alfred Iverson's brigade of Confederate infantry had arrived. The unit had suffered severe losses at Gettysburg, but still mustered 600 men. Unleashing heavy volleys, they cut the West Virginians to pieces. Thirty-four of the forty troopers were killed or wounded. The other six men were captured. The losses in the 18th Pennsylvania were just as severe.[37]

Confederate infantry also occupied the market house and fired away at the shattered Union forces. Residents took shelter in their basements or under beds. Sometime during the fighting, a soldier glanced to the rooftops looking for the enemy. He saw "Little Heiskell", the city's weather vane, outlined against the sky, and blasted away. One bullet struck it in the center and caused it to spin rapidly in all directions.[38]

Street fighting, and engagements between small groups of soldiers, occurred for nearly six hours. Kilpatrick began to realize that street fighting was folly, and slowly began to withdraw. This was hastened when a captured Confederate said that large numbers of Confederates were approaching the city. As the firing died down, residents and doctors began to minister to the wounded and dying in the streets of Hagerstown.

Earlier, when Jeb Stuart rode into Hagerstown, Confederates already in Hagerstown, mistook him for a Union officer and fired some shots in his direction.

When Kilpatrick entered Hagerstown, it was held by just the two small Confederates brigades of Chambliss and Robertson. Looking back, one wonders if a lightning attack by Kilpatrick, early in the morning, may have brought a wedge between Imboden on the banks of the Potomac, and Lee's approaching army. As the day lengthened, much of Stuart's cavalry was present, as well as Iverson's brigade and some troops from John Bell Hood's command. The arrival of fresh Confederate cavalry and infantry enabled Stuart to exert pressure on Kilpatrick's flank and rear.[39]

Earlier in the day, Colonel B. F. Eshleman and the Washington Artillery arrived in Williamsport. It was indeed early, 3:00 a.m. The gunners had been riding for three days. The men and the horses had suffered greatly. In fact, they had been on the march for forty-two hours without rest or food. "Reaching Williamsport, they were ordered to the junction of the Hagerstown-Boonsboro road."[40]

As the cavalry fought, the infantry of both armies plodded on in the rain. "The windows of heaven opened, . . . the rain came in sheets and meadows were turned into swamps, then lakes."

CRISES AT WILLIAMSPORT—CSA

Early that morning, John Imboden, on the banks of the Potomac at Williamsport received the news of the approach of a large Union cavalry force along with three batteries. These were the troopers of John Buford, Judson Kilpatrick, and Huey's brigade of Gregg's cavalry. Later, Imboden learned that the force consisted of 3,000 men in twenty-three cavalry regiments and eighteen cannon.

Imboden posted his cannon on the hills commanding the approaches to Williamsport. He ordered his troopers to fight from dismounted positions. They were assisted by all the able-bodied wagoners, who used the weapons of the wounded. In his preparations, Imboden was assisted by Colonel J. L. Black and Colonel William R. Aylett of Virginia. By noon he had 700 men in place, organized in companies of 100 men each. They were commanded by wounded line officers. Aylett held the right, and Black the left, with Imboden in the center.

Imboden says the enemy appeared in his front about 5 p.m. They were on both sides of the Hagerstown and Boonsboro roads. "Every man under my command understood that if we did not repulse the enemy we should all be captured, and General Lee's army be ruined. . . . The fight began with artillery on both sides." The Confederate fire was very rapid and slowed the Union advance. Imboden's artillery ran out of ammunition. The cannoneers had to wait while a fresh supply was ferried across the Potomac. The boxes were broken open with axes. When the Confederate artillery reopened, Imboden advanced his line to make a show of force.[41]

Night was approaching when a courier galloped up bringing a message from Fitzhugh Lee. Imboden urged "Hold your own, I am coming in half an hour with three thousand fresh men."[42] The good news passed along the line was met with cheers from those in the front lines. Off in the distance, there was the sound of other guns. It was to the rear and right on the Hagerstown Road. This was Stuart approaching from Hagerstown. Lee's men were coming from Greencastle. "That settled the contest. The enemy broke to the left and fled by the Boonsboro road. It was too dark to follow."[43]

Fitz Lee and staff stopped to confer with Imboden. It was almost a fatal mistake. An enemy shell exploded in the midst, Lee and Imboden were fortunate to escape. Imboden captured about 125 men. He was pleased with the bravery of his men. "The wagoners fought so well that this came to be known as the wagoners' fight.[44] By extraordinary good fortune we had thus saved all of General Lee's trains. A bold charge at any time before sunset would have broken our feeble lines, and then we should all have fallen easy prey to the Federals."[45] For this action as well as succeeding in getting the wagon train to the Potomac, Imboden ranks as the best Confederate leader on the roads from Gettysburg.

Between 4:00 and 5:00 p.m., the Union army pushed forward and burned many of the Confederate wagons loaded with plunder from Pennsylvania. Then from the cover of a woods, came the attack. John Buford advanced a large group of men and eight pieces of artillery. Dismounted men leveled the fences in their front. The Confederate pickets were recalled.

William Pegram, a brilliant young Confederate gunner, grasped the situation. He realized the position could not be held against a superior force. There were two choices: attack or retreat. To delay the Union advance, Pegram gave the order to attack. Although Company F of the 21st Virginia had but fifty-two men present for duty, they went forward, and even captured fifteen Yankees. Both sides brought up reinforcements. Some of the wounded grabbed weapons and rushed to support Company F.

John Worsham considered this action, F Company's best battle of the war. Just a mere handful of men stood between John Buford and Lee's wagons and main line of retreat. The handful had saved the day, keeping John Buford from reaching the riverbank in Lee's rear.

Company F lost four men. An additional loss was Captain Pegram of the artillery. His decision to make the attack may have been the order that saved Lee's army. The army mourned his loss. "Young, unassuming, but a true soldier, he was noted for his gallantry on many a battlefield." The next day, Pegram and the members of Company F were buried in Williamsport, "a city they had given their lives to win."[46]

John Buford gives this account of the attack from the Union perspective.

July 6, the whole division (the Reserve Brigade having joined the night before) marched at 4 a.m. towards Williamsport, to destroy the enemy's trains, which were reported to be crossing the Potomac into Virginia. At about 5 p.m., when near St. James College, the enemy's pickets were discovered, driven in, and preparations made to capture the town. The enemy was driven handsomely to within half a mile of his trains at the town, when he came out strong enough to prevent our further progress. General Merritt's brigade with Graham's battery was on the right, Colonel Gamble's (First) brigade on the left and Colonel Devin's (Second) brigade on the left as rear reserve. The enemy made an attack upon Gamble, who had posted his men under shelter and who held their fire until the rebel line came within short carbine range, when he opened upon it, doing terrible execution and driving it back to its stronghold. This was repeated with similar success. In Merritt's front the enemy made no direct attack, but were so obstinate that General Merritt could not dislodge them without too much sacrifice. The enemy, however, attempted to turn our right with a brigade of infantry. This attempt was most admirably foiled by General Merritt. While our hottest contest was in progress General Kilpatrick's guns were heard in the direction of Hagerstown, and as they drew nearer I directed him to connect with my right for mutual support. The connection was made, but was of no consequence to either of us. Just before dark Kilpatrick's troops gave way, passing to my rear by the right, and were closely followed by the enemy. It now being dark, being outnumbered, and the First and Reserve Brigades being out of ammunition, Devin was ordered to relieve Gamble and a portion of Merritt's troops. This being done, I ordered the command to fall back, Devin to hold his group until the entire road to Antietam was clear. Devin handsomely carried out his instructions, and the division bivouacked on the road to Boonsboro.

The expedition had for its object the destruction of the enemy's trains, supposed to be at Williamsport. This, I regret to say, was not accomplished. The enemy was too strong for me, but he was not punished for his obstinacy. His casualties were more than quadruple mine.

Colonel Chapman, with his regiment, dashed off to the road leading from Falling Waters to Williamsport, destroyed a small train of grain and Captain Graham fought his battery with marked ability and to the admiration of all witnesses. The officers and men behaved with their usual courage, displaying great unwillingness to fall back and requiring repeated orders before doing so.[47]

The Michigan cavalry lost heavily. During the action, Judson Kilpatrick sat on his horse, tapping his boot with his whip. Then he rode into the fray and led his men in an orderly withdrawal.

John Buford had less than 4,000 troopers under his command and Judson Kilpatrick had 3,500. The fighting was severe. Buford was unable to take Williamsport, and the outnumbered Confederates were unable to dislodge the Yankees in their counterattack. During the action, the Confederates were assisted by some of the cannon of the famed Washington Artillery from New Orleans.

William Gamble, commanding the 1st Brigade of Buford's cavalry, reports that three-fourths of his men dismounted to drive the enemy skirmishers back. The remaining fourth held the horses. Tidball's battery supported the Union troopers. Although outnumbered, the Union troopers had the advantage of being with carbines. The "dismounted men were under the immediate command of the gallant and lamented Major Lawrence Medill, Eighth Illinois Cavalry, who fell mortally wounded."[48]

Gamble's men held their position until dark when they were relieved by Colonel Devin's brigade" and ordered to fall back to Jones's Crossroads, in the direction of Boonsborough." The position was reached about midnight.[49]

Gamble's troopers had pressed the Confederate right between the Boonsboro-Williamsport Roads and the river. The brigade attempted a flanking movement. The 3rd Indiana, under Major John L. Beveridge, raced through Downsville, thence to the road leading to Williamsport. There they captured seven Rebel wagons and 100 prisoners.

The Confederates launched a counterattack from the woods. Devin's brigade came up as reinforcements. Captain John C. Tiball's Battery opened with heavy fire and assisted in repulsing the Confederates.

CIVILIANS

Moisture-laden clouds hovered near the ground as the 11th Virginia Cavalry rode from Fairfield to Cavetown. They moved along steadily through Chewsville into the east end of Hagerstown. Then the troopers under Colonel Lunsford Lomax turned south into the town. Suddenly cheers were heard. The men came alive, and sought to determine the cause of the cheers.

The source of the cheers was a lovely young lady standing in the doorway of an old stone mill. Draped around her was a small flag containing the Stars and Bars of the Confederacy. Officers and men tipped their hats and offered regards. Captain McDonald of Company D spoke for the men, and requested a piece of the flag as a keepsake. The teenage girl removed the entire flag and gave it to the captain. He said he would use "the apron flag" as his colors as long as the unit was in Maryland. He held the flag aloft. There were more cheers. At that moment, Private James M. Watkins, also a young man, begged for permission to carry the new colors, saying he would guard them with his life. This was done. Watkins also held the flag high, and once again there were cheers. The 11th then rode away.[50]

The Rowland's lived north of Hagerstown. They were devout members of the Longmeadow Church of the Brethren and pacifists. Ann Rowland was 52 years old in the summer of 1863.

On the way to Gettysburg, Alfred Jenkins and his cavalry visited the Rowland farm and helped themselves to some of the livestock and crops. All the Rowland horses were taken with the exception of Old Jen, who was hidden in a storage cave. This might have worked, except Old Jen became lonely and began to neigh. Soldiers also took her. Mrs. Rowland went to see General Lee who was nearby. The General complimented her for her bravery and ordered the driving mare returned.

Although there is some question as to the exact time and location, according to church and family traditions, Lee camped near the church and the Rowland's on the way from Gettysburg. Mrs. Rowland again went to see General Lee. Apparently fearful that the pulpit Bible would disappear just like the one at the Dunker Church[51] at Antietam, she requested the Bible be given to her for safekeeping. It is said that Lee arose from his desk, near or in the Longmeadow Church, and said, "If it is left here General Lee pledges his honor that the Holy Word shall be kept safely and no harm will come to this place of worship." Lee was true to his word, and members of the congregation say that the general used their pulpit Bible during his morning devotions.[52]

—4—

Tuesday, July 7, 1863

That morning, Mr. Lincoln had a cabinet meeting. The president was weary, and sad. Reports from Gettysburg were sketchy. Meade was still near Gettysburg when he should have been at Hagerstown or Williamsport, cutting off Lee's escape route. Honest Abe said, "I don't like to complain. General Meade has won a great victory. But I'm afraid the officers are more interested in driving the rebels out of Maryland than they are in capturing them."[1]

While the cabinet meeting was in session, George Meade was heading south on the Old Frederick Road, riding from Gettysburg through Creagarstown and Utica. He was headed toward Frederick where just nine days earlier he had taken command of the Army of the Potomac.

There were many things on Meade's mind. He needed a good, loyal chief of staff. George preferred a man of his own selection. Dan Butterfield was Hooker's man. Temporarily Alfred Pleasonton, the cavalry chieftain, and G. K. Warren, an engineer officer, were chosen to handle the important duties.

When Meade reached Frederick late in the day, he found a festive mood. Riding in North Market Street he saw hundreds of flags with thirty-four stars fluttering in the breeze. Cheers and shouts of joy greeted the general and his staff, the infantrymen, and the rest of the Army of the Potomac. The elderly, and even some of the infirmed, were out in the street to see the victors. Frederick was rolling out the red carpet for a victorious army this July day in the summer of '63. Everybody wanted to see the general who had defeated Robert E. Lee. It was a great day in the life and history of Frederick.

There were several leading hotels in Frederick: the Dill House, a fashionable place near the Court House; the City Hotel on West Patrick Street; and the United States Hotel on the southwest corner of South Market Street and All Saints Street. The last named hotel was the one selected by General Meade for army headquarters. It was just across the street from the Baltimore and Ohio (B&O) Railroad Station, and thus very convenient for messengers and staff personnel.[2]

Inside the hotel, Meade resumed plans to trap Lee. However, he was interrupted several times. A group of ladies came to present him "with showers of wreaths and bouquets," along with praise. Rufus Ingalls, the quartermaster general of the army, then joined Meade in appealing to Washington to send fresh supplies of food and clothing to Frederick.[3]

General Meade was very happy with the reception in Frederick. Maybe Lincoln and General Halleck did not appreciate him; however, the citizens and local people, they were grateful. Meade did not like popular demonstrations. However, there is no question that the reception by the folks of Frederick boosted his morale. Writing home, General Meade said, "The people in this place have made a great fuss over me."[4] Unlike other generals who thrived on praise, Meade felt the praise was undeserved. Lee was still on Maryland soil, thirty miles away. He wanted to await developments. Then let the people cheer.

Fredericktown residents visiting the general found him simple, direct, and considerate. In many ways he was like "Stonewall" Jackson, very plain and down to earth. Meade was forty-seven in the summer of '63, but he looked to be sixty-five. He was tall with a gray beard, and wore an old slouched hat. A blue blouse was tucked into corduroy pants. Some who had seen Meade on the twenty-seventh and twenty-eighth of June felt that he had aged thirty years during the previous days.

During the evening, Meade was serenaded by the people of Frederick. Great crowds thronged South Market Street to say, "Thank you, General." And fifty miles away, crowds gathered on the lawn of the White House to serenade Mr. Lincoln.

In Washington, the crowd called on Mr. Lincoln to give a speech, but he made only a few remarks. He praised the army, but did not mention any generals because he did not want to miss any of them. Some felt he should have at least mentioned the name of George Meade, for the new commander had just made the best showing of any general in the eastern theater of operations. Throughout the nation this July night, there were rallies, speeches, and fireworks. From the Atlantic to the Mississippi River, huge torchlike parades were held. Vicksburg had fallen; Lee had been driven from Gettysburg; maybe it would soon be over.

As the seventh drew to a close in Frederick, Meade had supply problems. Rufus Ingalls had notified General Meigs in Washington on July 5, that a supply base was to be established in Frederick. Horses, forage, food, clothing, medical supplies, etc., were started at once for western Maryland. Ingalls did not arrive until late that Tuesday. Much to his dismay, he learned that General French had tied up all railroad traffic, stopping the B&O trains for a time. These had brought reinforcements, but French would not let them go on to Harpers Ferry. Instead of permitting the men to dismount, and sending the trains back for supplies, French kept the men on the train and this kept the cars idle.

Ingalls became very angry about the situation. He fussed at the railroad because they did not have a dispatcher with power and authority in Frederick. He wired Washington to keep the fresh horses and rush food and personal items for the men. Monocacy Junction became a very busy place. Trains came, unloaded, and wagons carrying precious cargo rumbled through the streets of Frederick heading for Jefferson and Middletown. Shoes and boots were badly needed. Tramping from Fredericksburg to Gettysburg and back, left many men shoeless.

Once again Meade was criticized for taking the long road after Lee. He needed supplies and Monocacy Junction, near Frederick, was the ideal base. Good roads connected him with Washington and Baltimore, and there was the railroad.

In addition to the supply problem, the rain and mud continued to play havoc with the troop movements. Another two days would pass before the batteries of the I and VI Corps could join the infantry, then thousands of horses would have to be rested.

Mr. Lincoln was hungry for a crushing victory. Later in summer, the general went to Washington to confer with the president and his cabinet. During the conversations, Lincoln turned to Meade and said, "Do you know, General, what your attitude toward Lee for the week after Gettysburg reminded me of?"

Lincoln answered, "I'll be hanged if I could think of anything else but an old woman trying to shoo her geese across the creek."[5]

I CORPS—USA

Marching from March Creek, through Emmitsburg, the troops of the I Corps found members of the VI Corps, resting after their march from Fairfield. Throughout the day, the members of the corps, with their decimated ranks, marched through Franklinville, Mechanicstown, and Catoctin Furnace.[6]

Somewhere near Lewistown, members of the 13th Massachusetts were serenaded by a group of pretty, bright-eyed girls standing on fence rails. The lasses sang "The Battle Cry of Freedom." They were dressed in red, white, and blue. The veterans' eyes "moistened as they listened to the pretty little creatures sing." It was a sad experience, too. One hundred eighty-five men had tramped through the village on the roads to Gettysburg. Ninety-nine were present to hear the girls sing.[7]

In Lewistown, the column turned to the west toward Catoctin Mountain. Some officer had studied a map, but not the terrain. They were headed for Hamburg Pass that led to the crest of the mountain, to Bellsville, and thence into Middletown Valley. The climb, says Henry Kieffer, was "steeper and steeper. While the darkness was deeper and deeper."[8]

Someone must have alerted Charles Wainwright about the steep climb and difficult road. Most of the artillery continued to Frederick and apparently used the Shookstown Road. Teams were doubled to pull the cannon up the mountain. It was 10:00 p.m. before all the batteries arrived. It poured all night.[9]

Long marches were the order of the day for the Army of the Potomac. Heavy rains had made the roads deplorable, and then toward evening, the heavens opened again. With their long marches, the Army of the Potomac achieved in one day, what Meade expected to require two or three days.

Elements of the XI Corps made the longest march from Emmitsburg to Middletown, thirty-two to thirty-four miles, depending on their start. Slocum and the XII Corps tramped twenty-nine miles from near Littlestown to Walkersville.

III CORPS—USA

The III Corps began the march from Gettysburg with a new commander. David Birney was now at the helm replacing the wounded Daniel Sickles. Alexander Humphreys was leading his division for the last time. Tomorrow he would become Meade's chief of staff. The route of the III Corps was to Mechanicstown, and south to Lewistown. Humphreys had been ordered to take Hamburg Pass to the Middletown Valley. However, the order was countermanded due to traffic congestion and poor roads.[10] Drummer boy Bardeen purchased a good munch of green peas in Emmitsburg. The price was ten cents.[11]

The 141st Pennsylvania brought up the rear of the III Corps. They found the march slow and difficult. The heavy rains had made "the whole country a sea of mud."[12] Reaching Mechanicstown, they received good news, the fall of Vicksburg was announced.[13]

V CORPS—USA

The V Corps broke camp at Marsh Creek and started south. Their destination was Frederick, nearly twenty miles away. "The 20th Maine marched . . . through the rain, with the dark sky overhead, . . . and heavy mud underfoot." They made camp, soaked to the skin on wet and muddy ground. There was a chill in the dampness, but the vermin crawling in their woolen uniforms, and over their skin, were not bothered.

The men of George Sykes sloshed through the mud on their route south on the Old Frederick Road. It was a dreary day with a heavy mist, and sometimes an occasional shower. Camp was made at Utica, a village settled shortly after the Revolutionary War by Hessian prisoners brought from Saratoga to Frederick and then paroled.[14] Some of the units marched thirty miles in nineteen hours. The order to "fall out" was given at 10:00 p.m. At that moment there was a heavy downpour. The earth was soaked, so the men tried to sleep, wet and cold. The V Corps was camped between Utica and High Knob. High Knob is now a park and overlooks the lovely Middletown Valley.

VI CORPS—USA

This was another memorable day in the life and history of the VI Corps. After spending the night in Emmitsburg, the troops began marching southward through Catoctin Furnace and Lewistown. Then they turned to the west and Catoctin Mountain. The corps was supposed to cross the mountain at Hamburg Pass. The road is difficult to traverse in 1998, and was much worse in 1863, especially with all the wind, rain and mud.

Nelson Hutchinson and the rest of the troops never forget the night.

> The darkness was intense . . . nothing could be seen. Mounted officers could not see the men in the ranks. You could not see who was beside you, if anyone was there. We had to make way for the artillery. They got stuck, while we ended up scattered in the woods. Finally men who could stagger no further, lay down in the pouring rain.[15]

For the men in the ranks, the horrors and agony of this night would never be equaled. Rain had fallen almost continuously since the afternoon of July 4. Wagons and artillery were stalled in the mud, when a guide offered to take the VI Corps through a shortcut in the mountains. Like most shortcuts, it turned out to be less than the best. The troops named it "Sedgwick's Pass." Others called it "Mount Misery." There was but a single track, then the rocks. The rain had washed the dirt covering off the road bed. The troops were headed for Hamburg Pass. It was a rough trip during the day, let alone in the rain and mud of a July night. "The night was pitch dark and the rain pouring.[16]

The artillery was following the infantry. They got part way towards the pass, departing from the Frederick-Mechanicstown Road near Lewistown. Soon officers realized their task was impossible. In the midst of the rain, darkness, and mud they had to unhitch the horses, turn them around, turn the cannon around, and reverse their course. The situation produced short fuses, and angry tempers. Soon the black of night was blue with profane curses. Everything was game, the weather, Bobbie Lee, General Sedgwick, the animals, war, etc. The men of the VI Corps would always remember two nights in the Gettysburg Campaign: (1) The forced march from Manchester, Maryland to Gettysburg, eighteen miles in thirty-six hours, and (2) the trek in the rain to Hamburg Pass.[17]

North of Turner's Gap there were several passes across the mountain. Harmon's Pass, linking Mechanicstown and Smithsburg, was ruled out because the Army of the Potomac was to rendezvous in the Middletown Valley. South of Harmon's was Hamburg, a very rough pass. Next was the Shookstown Pass near Frederick. This was steep but not impassable, and was used throughout the war by Union troops.

Union troops marching through Middletown in 1862 on the way to Antietam. Scene repeated July 1863.

Frank Leslie's *Illustrated*, October 1862

XI CORPS—USA

This was an extremely long day for the XI Corps. They broke camp at 3:30 a.m. and marched several miles in the dark. Hours later, at 8:00 p.m., the head of the column reached Middletown. Crossing the mountain was most difficult. Most of the horses "were broken down by previous fatigue, only one division, (General) Schurz's division succeeded in reaching Middletown." General Howard, in his official report, notes that the First and Second Divisions remained near High Knob.

The XI Corps departed Frederick by way of what is now Fourth Street to the hamlet of Shookstown and crossed Catoctin Mountain at Shookstown Pass. This route was often used during the Civil War.

Thus the Army of the Potomac used Hamburg Pass, Shookstown Pass, and the main route on the Old National Road to cross into Middletown Valley.

XII CORPS—USA

The XII Corps was on the road at 4:00 a.m. Some of the troops covered twenty-nine miles. Some reached Frederick, while the rear of the column was in Walkersville.

The infantry broke ranks to permit the artillery to use the road. Marching in wet, muddy fields was most difficult.

ARMY OF NORTHERN VIRGINIA—CSA

Longstreet's command strengthened their lines near Hagerstown, while Ewell and A. P. Hill continued on the roads from Gettysburg. The Second Corps marched through Leitersburg, a village named after Jacob Leiter. It was probably the biggest day in the history of the German farming village. Camp was made on the Greencastle Pike, one and a half miles from Hagerstown. Robert Rodes was south of the road to Leitersburg, while Jubal Early was on the Greencastle Pike. Edward Johnson was near the crossing of the Antietam, in the rear. Heavy rains descended in the afternoon and continued well into the night. It was difficult sleeping in the mud.

Twenty miles away, General James Longstreet was happy to state that the Confederates had deployed their lines to cover what remained of the pontoon bridge at Falling Waters and the ford at Williamsport. Infantry and artillery batteries were in position. Longstreet noted that the enemy had the "longer outer curve of the battle line, while the Confederates were on the concentrating inner lines."

BUFORD'S CAVALRY—USA

John Buford sent more details to headquarters about the action on Monday:

> I attempted to take Williamsport yesterday, but found too large infantry and artillery. After a long fight I withdrew. . . . Heavy forces were coming into Williamsport all night. There are good many wagons at Williamsport. There is no bridge. . . . Troops and wagons are being ferried across in two flat boats. . . . I can do nothing with the enemy except observe him. There is nothing at Sharpsburg.[18]

Buford and Kilpatrick thus held the mountain passes, and guarded the approaches for the Army of the Potomac to advance.

South of Boonsboro, in Pleasant Valley, General William French occupied Crampton's Gap near Burkittsville, and sent a force to occupy Maryland Heights. This move was designed to prevent Stuart or any other Confederate force from attempting to turn the left flank of the Union army.

—5—

𝔚𝔢𝔡𝔫𝔢𝔰𝔡𝔞𝔶, 𝔍𝔲𝔩𝔶 8, 1863

Writing from Headquarters, Army of the Potomac, George G. Meade relayed good news to his wife.

Frederick, July 8, 1863

I arrived here yesterday; the army is assembling at Middletown. I think we shall have another battle before Lee can cross the river, though from all accounts he is making great effort to do so. For my part, as I have to follow and fight him, I would rather do it at once and in Maryland than to follow in to Virginia. I received last evening your letters of the 3rd and 5th inst., and am truly rejoiced that your are treated with such distinction on account of my humbler services. I see also that the papers are making a great deal too much fuss about me. I claim no extraordinary merit for this last battle, and would prefer waiting a little while to see what my career is to be before making any pretensions. I did and shall continue to do my duty to the best of my abilities, but knowing as I do that battles are often divided by accidents, and that no man of sense will say in advance what their results will be, I wish to be careful in not bragging before the right time. George is very well, thought both of us are a good deal fatigued with our recent operations. From the time I took command till today, now over ten days, I have not changed my clothes, have not had a regular night's rest, and many nights not a wink of sleep, and for several days did not even wash my face and hands, no regular food, and all the time in a great state of mental anxiety. Indeed, I think I have lived as much in this time as in the last thirty years. Old Baldy is still living and apparently doing well; the ball passed within half an inch of my thigh, passed through the saddle and entered Baldy's stomach. I did not think he could live, but the old fellow has such a wonderful tenacity of life that I am in hopes he will.

The people in this place have made great fuss with me. A few moments after my arrival I was visited by a deputation of ladies, and showers of wreaths and bouquets presented to me, in most complimentary terms. The street has been crowded with people, staring at me.[1]

Meade also received a letter from Washington. The sender was General Halleck, informing him that he had been appointed a brigadier general in the regular army, dating from July 3, the moment of "your brilliant victory at Gettysburg."[2]

I CORPS—USA

It was raining again, as the Iron Brigade began marching toward Middletown from Hamburg Pass. They passed through the lovely village of Harmony, and halted about 11:00 a.m. for lunch. The sun came out bright and warm. It was a most welcome sight. The warm rays helped dry the soaked uniforms, tents, and blankets.

At 3:00 p.m., the First Brigade of the First Division, of the I Corps, marching on the National Road crossed South Mountain at Turner's Gap, near the location of their action on September 14, 1862. The column halted at the western base of the mountain near Boonsboro.[3]

Charles Wainwright of the I Corps Artillery made two marches. The first was to Middletown. Camp was made on the banks of Catoctin Creek just west of the village. Men bathed themselves and cleaned equipment. Supply wagons arrived with clean clothing. This was a great blessing, as most of the men had gone nearly two weeks without a change of clothing. Wainwright ordered his battery commanders to wash carriages and harness. Later in the day, after the respite, the artillery was ordered to Turner's Gap.[4]

Prior to Gettysburg, the 4th U.S. Artillery had been the best dressed battery in the army. Now after days of marching, combat, dust and rain, their uniforms looked like rags.[5]

The II Corps, the unit that held the Union center against Pickett's charge, traveled from their camps along what is now Maryland Route 194, to Ceresville and the Monocacy River. Headquarters were established on the left bank of the river.[6]

Colonel Livermore thought the road from Woodsboro to Frederick was the best he had ever seen. He had spent the previous night "in a fine Maryland farmhouse which was used as headquarters." From the Monocacy, Livermore rode into Frederick to a barbershop. While he was getting his hair cut, someone stole his rubber coat from his saddle bags.[7]

Joseph Ward was impressed with the pastoral beauty of Woodsboro. Near the town, the column halted, and General Hays announced to the troops the news of the capture of Vicksburg. Cheers filled the air, and the streets of Woodsboro echoed the joyous news. The glad tidings eased the plight of marching in the rain. Reaching the Monocacy, General Alexander Webb made headquarters. The men were already soaked, so they jumped into the Monocacy and bathed.[8]

Grateful residents along the way brought food, water, and fruit to the soldiers.

V CORPS—USA

As the V Corps broke camp, officers related they were headed for Middletown and South Mountain. The 20th Maine would be retracing their steps from the previous September, when they had joined the Army of the Potomac at Antietam.

Bodies were stiff from the marches and dampness, nevertheless, it was on the road again, soldiers trudging wearily. There was little banter in the ranks. As they neared the Catoctin Mountain range, a tremendous thunder storm struck. The rain fell in torrents. It was one of the heaviest storms in memory. Daylight became as night. The thunder rolled, and the lightning flashed as the troops descended the mountain slope to Middletown Valley.

When night came, they camped close to South Mountain. In fact, the 20th Maine camped in the same field where tents were pitched in September 1862. "They drank from the same spring, washed in the same ditch." Some of them slept in a dry strawstack. The next day, they would resume the march after Bobbie Lee.

VI CORPS—USA

The VI Corps suffered many difficulties during July 7–8. Everything seemed to go wrong. First, there was the fifteen-mile march in a heavy rain. They had reached the foot of the mountain when darkness descended. The road to Hamburg Pass was barely more than a path. Jagged rocks were in the trail. Instead of marching four abreast, there was hardly room for two men. In addition to the "Mount Misery" title, some of the soldiers called it "Sedgwick's Pass."

When dawn of the eighth arrived, the soldiers were glad for a clearing trend. Someone discovered a mountain stream. The water was cold, but soldiers washed their faces and muddy clothing. One lad said, "We could recognize one another again." Later in the day, the VI Corps arrived in Middletown.

When the VI Corps headed south, Neill's Brigade had been left at Fairfield. Now assured that Lee had indeed left the area, Neill's men crossed at Fairfield Pass and reached Waynesboro. When they arrived in the evening, the residents turned out to give them a gala welcome. The soldiers were given sliced bread, cooked meats, pies, "and almost everything in the eatable line."[9]

XI CORPS—USA

Oliver O. Howard continued to move the XI Corps toward Middletown. He reported that the mission was accomplished before 11:00 a.m. "The road over the mountain near High Knob was steep, narrow, and very rocky. . . . It was with the greatest difficulty that the artillery and trains were brought over."[10] Because of the slow movement and clogged roads, the V Corps was ordered to take another route, rather than following the XI. High Knob is just north of the Shookstown Pass.

Two hours later, an order was received ordering the XI Corps to Boonsboro. The Third Division "had executed the movement at 5 p.m."[11] At the time, John Buford reported that his cavalry was hard pressed. He needed infantry support. The Third Division was immediately sent forward, while the First and Second Divisions, along with the artillery, were placed on the right and left of the National Pike on the western slope of South Mountain. When the Confederates saw the Union infantry, they retired. However, this was only after the Third Division had gone a mile beyond Boonsboro.

The XI Corps remained in position near Boonsboro on July 9. While in camp every effort was "made to supply shoes and clothing" so badly needed by the soldiers.[12]

BUFORD'S CAVALRY—USA

John Buford "had a very rough day of it."[13] Early that morning, a strong enemy force, consisting of Stuart's cavalry, and artillery advanced on Buford's position. They pressed him toward Boonsboro. "Toward night, I turned the tables upon them, and drove them across the Antietam toward Hagerstown and Williamsport. You never saw the division behave better. My loss is not heavy."[14]

Buford continued by saying:

> The artillery fire was very hot. All my fighting had to be on foot. The river is five feet higher than before and rising. I have drawn closer to this place (Boonsborough) to sleep. . . . There are no rebs this side of Antietam; none on the old battle ground, and none of them at Sharpsburg. Plenty of them, however, can be found between Greencastle and Williamsport, and between Hagerstown and Williamsport. Hurrah for Vicksburg.[15]

Buford lamented that his trains had been delayed by the approach of the XI Corps.[16]

Gamble's Brigade had been deployed to the right of the National Road, on the crest of a ridge. His skirmishers were thrown forward to the edge of a woods. Eventually Gamble was flanked and had to give up the woods.

During the action on July 8, the Yankees opened a signal station at Washington's monument, east of Boonsboro. Some of the men cut away large stands of timber obstructing the view to the west. Two hours later, the signal men were spotting Confederates movements, and sending vital information to General Buford.

STUART'S CAVALRY—CSA

General Stuart says his cavalry was "thrown forward toward Boonsborough, . . . in order, by a bold demonstration to threaten an advance of the enemy, and thus cover the retrograde of the main body."[17]

Stuart also says that General Jones engaged Union troops on the National Road at the Beaver Creek Bridge. "An animated fight ensued, principally on foot, the ground being entirely too soft from recent rains to operate successfully with cavalry."[18] Three captured Union prisoners relayed the news that the main cavalry force "of the enemy was in our front."[19]

Later in the day, Stuart's troopers began to run low on ammunition. He had succeeded in his mission. He realized Boonsboro could not be taken, and the town "was completely commanded by artillery in the mountain gap."[20] Thus, Stuart began to retire to Funkstown.

As the last Confederate regiment crossed Beaver Creek, a Union squadron galloped forward "as if to charge." The first North Carolina Cavalry waited and then opened heavy fire. They were supported by a Blakely gun of Chew's horse artillery. Chaos and confusion reigned in the Union ranks. The squadron turned and galloped toward its own lines, followed by shouts of derision from the Confederates. Stuart says, "Our command moved leisurely to the vicinity of Funkstown, and bivouacked for the night."

Stuart's task on the roads from Gettysburg was to stay between Meade's army and the Confederate position on the Potomac.[21]

SECOND CORPS—CSA

Ewell and his staff rode to General Lee's headquarters. Longstreet and A. P. Hill were also present. The generals, along with engineer officers and Jed Hotchkiss, went "on a reconnaissance of a line of defense from Hagerstown to Williamsport."[22] On that fine, warm, July day Jed and the generals were in the saddle all day, as well as the next day.

CIVILIANS

This was to have been the day Katherine Hewitt was to meet General John Reynolds in Philadelphia. The two would then journey to Lancaster to meet the general's family. However, John F. Reynolds had already taken the roads from Gettysburg in a casket, and now rested beneath the sod in Lancaster.

─6─
Thursday, July 9, 1863

The Army of Northern Virginia continued to converge on Williamsport and Falling Waters, preparing to cross the Potomac River as soon as the floods receded. Lee consolidated his lines of defense and there was the clash of cavalry.

From his headquarters at Middletown, Meade ordered the infantry corps to cross South Mountain, using Crampton's, Fox's, and Turner's Gaps. Some of his command marched without artillery, the horses had completely broken down. Union cavalry determined that Lee was indeed between Williamsport and Hagerstown. Confederate prisoners reported that supplies were being ferried across from the Virginia shore. They also said that the morale of the rebel army was high, and that the Army of Northern Virginia was ready for a good fight. Meade firmly expected a major battle to be fought in a few days, perhaps the decisive battle of the war.[1]

Meade also had a new chief of staff. Meade wanted a man of his choice to occupy that important post and chose Alexander A. Humphrey, who, a division commander, had commanded the III Corps in the absence of Dan Sickles. After the infantry had crossed the South Mountain range, Meade moved his headquarters westward to the Mountain House at the crest of Turner's Gap. The trains of the Army of the Potomac also used this pass. The Mountain House and Turner's Gap were not new to the troops, or to Meade. The pass had been of vital importance during the Maryland Campaign in 1862.

The I, VI, and XI Corps crossed the mountain at Turner's Pass. Three miles south, the III and V Corps crossed at Fox's Gap. They too proceeded to the western base of the mountain near the Mt. Carmel United Brethren Church. Meanwhile, farther to the south, the II and XII Corps tramped through Burkittsville and then crossed at Crampton's Gap.

I CORPS—USA

This was an easy day for the remnants of the Iron Brigade. They watched while the rest of the army poured through Turner's Gap. "The clatter of artillery wheels rolled over the roads. The material and force of a large army were pouring into the fields. The game of war went on with determination on one side and desperation on the other."[2]

Rufus Dawes who had fought at Turner's Gap in 1862 wrote another letter home. He felt the pursuit of Lee had been rapid. He was pleased with Meade's leadership. At long last, the Army of the Potomac was being well handled. Yet, "our men have suffered as never before. Almost half our men have marched barefoot for a week. . . . We have had severe rains since the battle. I have not slept in a dry blanket or had dry clothing on since crossing the Potomac. . . . If we can end this war right here, I will cheerfully abide the terrible risk of another battle."[3]

As headquarters was established at the Mountain House, Charles Wainwright spent most of the day there. He noted that everyone felt that John Buford was the best cavalry officer in the Army of the Potomac. Buford resembled John Reynolds in words and actions. Wainwright was disturbed that U. S. Grant was getting all the publicity for capturing Vicksburg, while the Army of the Potomac had yet to receive a letter of thanks from President Lincoln.[4]

II CORPS—USA

There is little in official or regimental accounts for this day. However, the II Corps broke camp northeast of Frederick, near Ceresville, crossed the Monocacy, and embarked on a long march. Charles Page, a member of the 14th Connecticut, states that his unit marched twenty-three miles that day, in addition to twenty miles the previous day. The route was south from Frederick to Jefferson, thence to Burkittsville, and Crampton's Gap. Late in the evening, they reached their destination at Rohrersville.[5]

III CORPS—USA

Meanwhile, drummer boy Bardeen and the rest of the III Corps were on the march. Bardeen was sick, but found consolation in the fact, "For the first time in three weeks we have got a pleasant day." The young man, along with soldier McArty of Company G, spent the night in a Maryland barn. The regiment crossed the Catoctin mountains through Fox's Gap.[6]

The 141st Pennsylvania was also on the march. They had spent the night at Fox's Gap. The men expected to make a night march, but instead they were given a welcome rest. The 141st was inspected, inventories made of equipment losses and materials on hand, and also a listing of those present for duty. This was done during the afternoon of the eighth while taking a break near Middletown. Then they moved on the scene of

Reno's action on September 14, 1862. The view from the mountain and the cool breezes made them feel good. There was an alarm during the night. A horse broke loose, ran through the bivouac area, and scared the troops. They thought it might be a Confederate cavalry raid.[7]

It was a chaotic day for the 17th Maine. They broke camp at 5:00 a.m., two miles east of Middletown, marched through the lovely German farming village, and west of town pitched their tents. At 5:00 p.m., "the general sounded" and within the hour the men were on the road again. After a short march they halted and made another camp. Six miles, two stops, and two camps was their record for the day. On the way to Fox's Gap, they saw a rock with the simple inscription, "Here General Reno fell."

After the frustration of the day, the men looked forward to a night of rest on the Maryland mountainside, but it was not to be. The cattle accompanying the army stampeded during the night. Only the sentinels were awake and they were scared out of their wits. They were sure it was Stuart's cavalry so they sounded the alarm, and for awhile all was chaos and confusion. Most of the men did not know until daybreak what had happened. They thought the rebels were the culprits.[8]

VI CORPS—USA

John Sedgwick's command had a relatively short hike, just eight miles. From campsites west of Middletown, they departed at 5:00 a.m. Their destination was Boonsboro, a village named after Daniel Boone. Residents told the soldiers about cavalry actions west of the town. The VI Corps was ordered into a defensive line, which could also serve as a springboard for an attack. The corps was posted on a ridge with camp made in nice woods.[9]

XI CORPS—USA

Howard's corps remained in position near Boonsboro. Carl Schurz's division, occupying a forward position, was relieved. The troops strolled from their campsites to the nearby homes and farms seeking some good, wholesome food.[10]

V CORPS—USA

There is very little material on the occurrences in the V Corps for this July day. They crossed South Mountain at Fox's Gap and camped near Mt. Carmel Church, ready to proceed to Keedysville, then to the Upper Bridge over the Antietam and Bakersville.

XII CORPS—USA

Henry Warner Slocum's report for the day is brief. "We crossed South Mountain at Crampton's Pass, and encamped near Rohrersville."[11] A. S. Williams says simply, "We advanced toward Rohrersville."[12]

From the Mountain House, Meade penned his orders for the next day. The II and XII Corps were to advance from the Rohrersville area, through Keedysville, and move toward Bakersville.

The V Corps was to move by Devil's Backbone, (Maryland Route 68), toward Jones's Crossroads. A guide was to be furnished. The III Corps was to follow the V Corps. Sedgwick and the VI Corps was to take position on the north side of Beaver Creek. Meade would establish headquarters near Devil's Backbone at the III Corps.

CAVALRY ACTION AT BEAVER CREEK

Jeb Stuart says that the action on July 8 "administered a quietus . . . on the ninth." Jeb says his cavalry "kept the position in front of Funkstown assigned to it the night before."[13]

John Buford reports that he attacked the enemy "at 4 p.m. and drove him handsomely about two miles."[14]

Thomas Devin says that at 5:30 p.m. he crossed Beaver Creek "to carry the crest, . . . and feel the enemy's position. The men of the command advance as dismounted skirmishers, and with a battery sent to support them, drove the enemy back.[15]

While the infantry continued to march, and the cavalry rested in western Maryland, an ambulance reached an elegant home in Washington. It contained a feverished and pale young officer, Captain Ulric Dahlgren, USV. He was near death, traveling from Hagerstown to Washington. Dahlgren was carried to an upstairs bedroom at the home of his parents, Admiral and Mrs. John Dahlgren. There by the light of a flickering lamp, his leg was amputated.

Apparently, one of the first visitors was President Abraham Lincoln. Soon another visitor arrived. This was the Honorable Edwin M. Stanton, secretary of war. He brought the news that Captain Dahlgren, as the result of a promotion, was now Colonel Dahlgren.

About this time, Admiral Dahlgren was in the process of constructing a naval gun factory. They were about ready to lay the cornerstone. A question arose about the burial of young Dahlgren's amputated leg. A decision was made to bury the leg in a box in the cornerstone of the new naval gun factory. An inscription was added:

WITHIN THIS WALL IS DEPOSITED THE LEG OF COL. ULRIC DAHLGREN, USV, WOUNDED JULY 6, 1863, WHILE SKIRMISHING IN THE STREETS OF HAGERSTOWN WITH THE REBELS AFTER THE BATTLE OF GETTYSBURG.

CONFEDERATES

John Imboden shares some interesting experiences from the banks of the Potomac. He says that by July 9, his command had ferried 4,000

Ulric Dahlgren

National Archives and The Cracker Barrel,
Hagerstown, Md.

Union prisoners and some officers across the river. These men were headed for Staunton, and thence to Libby Prison in Richmond. They were guarded by a single regiment of Confederate infantry, the 62nd Virginia.

When Imboden was assigned the task of taking the wounded and the prisoners to the Potomac, Lee expressed grave concern that before Imboden could reach Winchester, Federal cavalry would cross at Harpers Ferry, "intercept and capture my guard and release the prisoners."[16]

Prior to leaving the banks of the Potomac, Imboden had a conference with Lee "at his headquarters near Hagerstown." He was very much troubled by the tardiness in preparing the pontoon bridge. Colonel James L. Corley was called in. Lee ordered him to place Major John Harman, formerly of Jackson's staff, to conduct the task. A man of Harman's great energy and resolve was needed. Harman took charge of the work with his usual zeal. The warehouses along the Chesapeake and Ohio Canal at Williamsport were torn down and hauled downstream to Falling Waters. Harman achieved this in just twenty-four hours. He found joists to go along with planking and the construction of the pontoons was under way.

FIRST CORPS—CSA

Randolph Shotwell crossed the Potomac from Williamsport to "Ol Virginny." Prisoners and guards were ferried across the river, twenty-five at a time. The river was full, muddy, and the current very swift. The crossing was dangerous. The boat creaked as it made the crossing.[17]

The Maryland shore was jammed. There were large groups of Union prisoners waiting to be taken to Staunton. Wagons, ambulances, artillery, horses, and mules were also waiting to be ferried across. In the background could be seen the spires of Williamsport. They pointed to peaceful skies. Shotwell pondered the difference from the crossing on the roads to Gettysburg. The tide of the Confederacy had been at its height, now it was receding. The Army of Northern Virginia was not crushed, but badly wounded. Union cavalry was nipping at their heels. Everybody noticed the contrast. Off in the distance there was artillery fire. Union and Confederate cavalry were engaged north of the river.[18]

J. F. K. Caldwell was very much impressed with the Confederate wagons waiting to be ferried across. He had never seen so many vehicles.

Artilleryman Moore stated that the river was two feet above flood stage. There was no way anyone could wade across.[19]

Robert E. Lee conferred with John Imboden about all the fords from Williamsport to Cumberland. Prior to Imboden's departure, General Lee had a question, "Tell me, does it ever stop raining around here?"[20]

—7—

Friday, July 10, 1863

George G. Meade took up the pen and wrote to his wife on this July day. Lee had not yet crossed the Potomac. Meade felt Lee had no intention of doing so, and thought that combat was imminent. He hoped for victory; felt the people had been deluded by Gettysburg and now expected miracles from him. He realized that the enemy was still capable of major action.

Henry Halleck was not satisfied. Message after message arrived from Washington, "Press and destroy the enemy. You have given the enemy a stunning blow at Gettysburg, follow it up and give him another before he can cross the Potomac."[1] Another communiqué arrived, "This opportunity must not be lost. The President is urgent and anxious that your enemy should move against him by forced marches."[2]

Meade, in the field closer to the action, replied that scouts found Lee crossing the river slowly. Meade added, "so long as the river is unfordable, the enemy cannot cross. . . . The enemy extends from Hagerstown to Williamsport. . . . Pickets are advanced to the Hagerstown-Sharpsburg Pike, on the general line of the Antietam. We hold Boonsboro, and our pickets four miles in front, . . . are in contact with the enemy's pickets. My army is assembling slowly; the rains . . . have made all roads but pikes almost impassive. Artillery and trains are stalled."[3]

The commanding general lamented that many of his men had been barefooted. However, a fresh supply of shoes had arrived at Frederick Junction on July 8, and were immediately sent to the front. "The spirit of the army is high. The men are ready and willing to make any exertion to push forward."[4]

As soon as the troops were resupplied, especially the artillery and cavalry, Meade desired to move against Lee and settle the issue on the north bank of the Potomac in Maryland. He hoped through "Providence and the bravery of my men to settle the question."[5] Realistically, Meade said, "I expect to find the enemy in a strong position, well covered with artillery, and I do not desire to imitate his example at Gettysburg and assault a position when the chances are so greatly against success."[6]

80

At 1:00 p.m., Meade telegraphed Halleck:

This information received today indicates that the enemy occupy positions extending from the Potomac, near Falling waters, through Downsville to Funkstown and to the northeast of Hagerstown, Ewell's Corps being to the northeast of Hagerstown, Longstreet's at Funkstown and A. P. Hill's on their right. These positions they are said to be entrenching.

I am advancing on a line perpendicular to the line from Hagerstown to Williamsport, and the army will this evening occupy a position extending from the Boonsboro and Hagerstown Road, at a point one mile beyond Beaver Creek, to Bakersville, near the Potomac. Our cavalry advance this morning drove the enemy's cavalry, on the Boonsboro Pike, to within a mile of Funkstown, when the enemy deployed a large force, and opened a fire from heavy guns (20-pounders).

I shall advance cautiously on the same line tomorrow until I can develop more fully the enemy's position and force upon which my future operations will depend. . . . [7]

Then it was Halleck's turn to vacillate. At 9:00 p.m. today, he told Meade, "I think it will be best for you to postpone a general battle till you can concentrate all your forces and get up all your reserve and reinforcements. I will push on the troops as fast as they arrive." Halleck suggested sending staff officers to the Monocacy rail junction to expedite matters. The new men were to be hurried forward by forced marches. Halleck admonished against partial combats and urged Meade to hit Lee with the full weight of his forces.[8]

I CORPS—USA

On Friday, elements of the I Corps and the artillery moved towards the village of Beaver Creek and Wagner's Crossroads. Charles Wainwright describes the situation:

The right of our corps, and I know of none beyond it in that direction, is about a quarter of a mile from a small village, and mill. We have a good position here, if our flanks are only taken care of, but I do not suppose that there is a possibility of Lee's attacking us. The men, I suppose by the advice of their officers or at any rate with their aid and consent, commenced piling up rails and digging earth the instant they were formed in line; even before orders came down from General Newton to do so. I was sorry to see so much anxiety to make themselves secure; it does not speak will for the morale of the men. I fear they are more willing to be attacked than they are to attack, which is not a good sign just now, for if there is any more fighting at all we must be the attacking party. Perhaps this feeling is not so much to be wondered at, when one takes into consideration the last three battles, and the tendency of the defensive, and wish to be always in that position.

There is a difference between the people of Maryland and those of Pennsylvania. A man of some fifty or more stood looking at our men pull down the fences to start their breastworks, and carrying off the sheaves of wheat just cut here for their beds. Having a fellow-feeling for the owner as a brother farmer, I spoke to the man and said it was hard on the owner of the land to destroy his crops and fences so. "Oh," says he, "you may destroy my whole farm if you will only whip the rebels." If the eastern Marylanders are the most bitter of the rebels, those west of Frederick are the truest Union people I have met with anywhere. This same willingness to sacrifice and give was apparent through this country in the Antietam campaign as well as in this one; their kindness was shown to the men as well before as after our victories.

The weather has been muggy, with more or less fine rain ever since the battle. It is not enough wet to interfere with us, save that the fields are very muddy, but it prevents the farmers from getting in their grain, and you can hardly stop the men from taking the sheaves to sleep on when the ground is so nasty. . . .[9]

The famed Iron Brigade took the National Pike to a point near Funkstown. There, east of the road and half a mile from Beaver Creek, they started to throw up entrenchments. Some soldiers disliked the spade work, but they knew that a pile of dirt is mighty good protection against shot and shell.[10]

The men from the mid-west remained behind the earthen barricades until Sunday. Colonel Morrow was exhausted from the campaign. In a few days he would take a sick leave.

The men in the ranks were saying the Meade should destroy Lee. Yet the two armies were pretty close in size and strength. The victory had cost the Army of the Potomac dearly. Meade looked upon Lee as a wounded lion, capable of turning and inflicting great damage if pursued too vigorously.

II CORPS—USA

Accounts for the day are sketchy. The march was from Rohrersville to Keedysville in the Antietam Valley, thence northward to Bakersville. Some members of the 14th Connecticut apparently stopped at the farm of John Hoffman. This had been a large hospital after the Battle of Antietam.

The weather cleared in the morning, but the heat and humidity returned in the afternoon. Several men in the First Massachusetts suffered sunstrokes.[11] Along the route from Keedysville to Bakersville, they saw many reminders of the Maryland Campaign: weathered headboards with names scrawled upon them, beginning to fade away under the exposure to the elements.[12] They also saw some bones protruding from shallow graves.

V CORPS—USA

Elements of the V Corps took Stonewall Jackson's way. Currently Maryland Route 68, leading from Boonsboro to Williamsport, remains virtually unchanged from the days of '63.[13] The trains were left at the Mountain House in Turner's Gap. Marsena Patrick did not expect any action any time soon. He was sure Lee "was in a strongly entrenched position."[14]

Among those tramping southward, was the 20th Maine and their famed leader, Colonel Joshua Lawrence Chamberlain. His men had anchored the left of the Union line. On July 2, the 20th fought a classic small unit action and saved the Union army from repeated attacks by the 15th Alabama and other Confederate units. On July 10, they became a part of the infantry committed to support the Union cavalry at Funkstown. Two more members of the regiment were killed and six wounded.

Just prior to being committed to the action, the Third Brigade of the First Division of the V Corps had formed in a field near Boonsboro. They were to march by in review. Then it was announced to the troops that their beloved commander, Colonel Strong Vincent, had been promoted to brigadier general. When Vincent was marching at the head of his column near Hanover, Pa., he had said "how glorious it would be to die for your country." Near the position of the 20th Maine on Little Round Top, Vincent had been mortally wounded. The troops cheered when the news of his promotion was announced. Sadly, they did not know that Vincent had expired from his wounds two days earlier at Gettysburg. When the news of his death reached the troops in the field, Chamberlain said, "I grieve for him much."[15]

VI CORPS—USA

The VI Corps advanced from Beaver Creek toward Funkstown. One of the veterans wrote:

> The entire operation . . . took place in one of the richest and finest agricultural regions of Maryland, and the necessary destruction of grain and crops was immense. Untold acres of the finest wheat, nearly ripe for the harvest, were trampled by the lines of battle, by marching columns or wagons and artillery parks. The residents of Washington County may have exclaimed, "From friend and foe alike deliver us."[16]

During the action, Colonel Lewis A. Grant's brigade of Vermont troops from Howe's division, was committed to the action. Nine members of the brigade were killed, and fifty-nine wounded. The brigade had spread out as skirmishers on a two-mile front.

As Thomas Hyde rode into the village, he saw a lovely girl waving two Confederate flags. Her eyes melted when she saw Tom's handsome friend Andrews. In a few moments she was talking with the two Yankees. She said she had ridden forty miles to deliver messages to Confederate leaders. She was honest and the two members of the VI Corps respected her allegiance to a different cause. They were also impressed with her beauty. They named her "The Funkstown Traitoress."[17]

Jacob Stonebraker, a resident of Funkstown, like the young woman, was very sympathetic toward the South. In fact, earlier in the war he had been imprisoned at Fort McHenry.

XI CORPS—USA

The XI Corps was in and around Boonsboro. They saw their comrades in the I and VI Corps, move on toward Beaver Creek, almost midway between Boonsboro and Funkstown. The day had hardly begun, when General Howard was ordered to report to John Sedgwick at Beaver Creek. Moving out, the XI Corps arrived on the scene at 4:30 p.m., and went into position on the right of the VI Corps, "near Hagerstown and Smoketown road two and a half miles from Funkstown."[18] Artillery fire could be heard. This was from the major engagement at Funkstown.[19]

Earlier in the day, from his headquarters near Boonsborough (his spelling), General Howard extended his thanks to the men of the corps "for what has been done during the last month. . . . You have now met the enemy . . . you have done your duty." Howard continued by saying:

> The Eleventh Corps, as a corps, had done well—well in marching, well in fighting; the sacrifices it had made will not be forgotten. . . . Now, we must make one more effort. Let there be no wavering, no doubt. . . . Our cause is right and our success is sure.[20]

XII CORPS

Henry Slocum and the XII Corps marched from Rohrersville to Bakersville, using from Keedysville the road running to the northwest to the Hagerstown Road. They passed over the same Upper Bridge they crossed on the night of September 16, 1862, in their approach march to the East Woods at Antietam.[21] After crossing the Antietam the XII Corps was drawn up in line of battle. However, nothing happened. Most of the corps tramped between ten and twelve miles on this warm day. Since Sunday, marching eastward from Gettysburg to Littlestown, thence south to Frederick, then west to the mountains, the troops had covered approximately seventy miles.[22]

CONFEDERATES

One of the officers, going to Lee's headquarters tent near Williamsport, was Edward P. Alexander. Lee asked the artillery officer about the strength of the defensive line. Alexander said, "It will hold General, it will hold." Alexander felt that Meade gave the Confederates three days to prepare the line of defense, three days without any real harassment, other than the cavalry action. The Georgia artilleryman said, "The enemy pursued as a mule goes on a chase of a grizzly bear—as if catching up to us was the last thing he wanted to do." However, Alexander felt that Lee seemed more anxious than at any time he had been in his presence. Lee's back was to the Potomac. No one could tell when the Potomac might recede, or when and if Meade might attack.

Jed Hotchkiss worked on his maps in the morning. Then he rode to General Lee's headquarters to place the defensive ridge on the map. All the corps commanders were present. The Yankees advanced to the Antietam Creek. "We had a cannonade and some skirmishing. This, of course, was the battle of Funkstown. Later in the day, the Second Corps retired to positions selected for them on the Williamsport Road. Jed escorted Ed Johnson's division to its position. Ewell's headquarters was established on the National Road, a mile and a half west of Hagerstown." Jed notes that it was very warm and the harvest was being cut. He adds, "We have destroyed much grain."[23]

Earlier, Colonel Fremantle mentions seeing Generals John Bell Hood and Wade Hampton in an ambulance near Waterloo, Pennsylvania. Hood later wrote:

> When the Confederate army fell back from Gettysburg, I followed our marching column in an ambulance, suffering very much from the wound received in my arm. In the same vehicle lay General Hampton, so badly wounded that he was unable to sit up, whereas I could not lie down. We journeyed together in this manner to Stuanton, a distance of some two hundred miles. Along the pike was seen our wounded, wending their way to the rear, and the noble women of Virginia, standing by the wayside to supply them with food, and otherwise administer to their wants.[24]

While the cavalry was dueling in the fields just east of Funkstown, the bulk of the Confederate infantry was in a defensive position a mile and a half west of Funkstown, and two miles south of Hagerstown. The left flank was on the Stocklager farm near the Downsville Pike. The Confederate line was approximately nine miles in length. Longstreet and the First Corps was on the right, A. P. Hill in the center, while Richard Ewell held the left flank.

After the engagement at Funkstown, there was more pick and shovel work for the Confederate infantry. They were sure that Meade would attack, perhaps the next morning. In fact, one of his soldiers, Robert Moore notes:

> Our cavalry had a heavy skirmish with the enemy this morning. . . . The weather is very hot and clear. Everything seems to indicate another engagement with the enemy at no distant day.[25]

Jeb Stuart was feeling a little better after his failures prior to Gettysburg. Writing to his wife he said:

> I write to say that God has mercifully spared me through many dangers and bloody fields. My cavalry has nobly sustained its reputation and done better and harder fighting than it ever has since the war. Pray without ceasing, that God will give us the victory.[26]

Lee was west of the road, nearer the river, with his left flank anchored in a very strong position along the Conococheague Creek. However, the defenses would not be completed for another two days.

BUFORD'S CAVALRY—USA

John Buford describes the day by saying:

> I have been fighting Fitzhugh Lee's, Hampton's, and Jones' Brigades; have driven them back upon Longstreet's whole corps which occupies the crest beyond the Antietam. . . . The whole of Lee's army is in the vicinity of Hagerstown, Jones' Crossroads, and extending toward Williamsport. His line will be along the Antietam. He has a large force in front of a bridge a mile below Funkstown. I don't care about going any farther just now. I will cease firing and try to watch their movements.[27]

Buford notes that he made his attack at 8:00 a.m. He lamented that the infantry of the VI Corps did not support him. Buford had carbines, but later in the day exhausted his ammunition.

William Gamble says that he advanced on Funkstown with dismounted skirmishers. His command opened with heavy musket and artillery fire into Funkstown. The First Brigade was in the center and on both sides of the National Pike. Calef's and Tidball's batteries were of great assistance. The cavalrymen occupied the heights above Funkstown. Gamble also was upset that infantry camped a mile behind the line of battle, pitched their tents, cooked supper, and did not come to the assistance of the embattled troopers. Gamble fell back because of lack of ammunition.[28]

Devin says that his brigade was halted when it was ascertained that Longstreet held the heights. Devin's brigade was on the east bank of the Antietam, close to both bridges across the stream.[29]

Young Jacob Stonebraker was an eyewitness to the engagement. He writes:

> The Battle of Funkstown
>
> Early in the morning, the first division of Major General Pleasonton's Cavalry, three brigades commanded by Brig. Gen. Buford were dismounted and formed in line as follows: The Reserve brigade, under Gen. Merritt, being on the right, the first under Col. Gamble in the center, and on both sides of the National Pike, the second under Col. Devin, on the left. This line was supported by two sections of Tidball's Light Horse Artillery. They

advanced up the Boonsboro Pike, driving the Confederate skirmishers before them and made a vigorous attack on Stuart's right, but were repulsed in fine style. Lt. Col. Witcher's dismounted cavalry, who were posted behind a stone fence, south of town, on the Hauck farm, sustained the brunt of this assault. These troops behaved gallantry and held their ground with unflinching tenacity.

Directly in front of Manly's battery was apiece of heavy timber, known as Stover's Woods. Buford's brigade occupied a portion of this timber.

Major General Sedgwick, commanding the Sixth Corps, says: "The enemy was posted near Funkstown. The Vermont Brigade, of the Second Division, were deployed as skirmishers, covering a front of over two miles, and during the afternoon repulsed three successive attacks made in line of battle."

The left of the Vermont brigade occupied a portion of Stover's Woods, its line running in a northwesterly direction through Stacklager's and Baker's land, its right resting on the road east of Stonebraker's barn. The Third New York Battery, under Capt. Harn and Company C, First Rhode Island battery, under Capt. Waterman, supported this line of infantry.

From these woods sharpshooters had been advanced in force to Stover's barn, which was about four hundred yards from the Confederate line. Col. White, with Anderson's brigade, pushed forward and drove the Federals out and from behind the barn through two open fields to the edge of the woods. Just as they reached the fence of the second field, Manly's battery exploded several shells among them, killing and wounding six of their number. It is bad enough to have to face the determined fire of the enemy, without having death lurking in your rear. This accident was caused by a defective fuse in the Confederate shells, and somewhat disconcerted and checked their advance, but they soon rallied, climbed a post and rail fence, and pushed halfway across a newly plowed corn field to within tow hundred yards of the woods in which Grant's and Buford's men were sheltered behind trees and large rocks. Here they met with a more determined resistance and sustained their heaviest loss. Gen. Fitz Lee, seeing no advantage to be gained by a further advance, ordered them to desist and return to their original position.

Manly's battery went into action about six p.m., and continued engaged until late in the afternoon. He shelled Stover's woods at a furious rate and fought Tidball's battery with effect, compelling them to change their position several times during the engagement. While the fight was raging on the right and center, a portion of Gen. Fitz Lee's brigade under Capt. Woolridge was hotly engaged on the left with Grant's right, finally compelling them to seek shelter in Stonebraker's woods, better known as "The Cedars."

From the garret of Mrs. Keller's house I saw a portion of this fight. The wounded were brought into town, and Mrs. Chaney's large dwelling was taken for a hospital. The surgeons had a table in the yard under some trees, and amputated arms and legs like sawing limbs from a tree. It was a horrible sight.

As fast as the wounded were dressed, they were carried into the house and laid on the floor in rows. The citizens administered to their wants; many died and their cries and suffering were distressing to behold. Simon Knode, an old Methodist deacon, added very much to the confusion as he prayed and sang to the dying.

On Sunday, after the battle, some of our citizens buried the Confederate dead that had been left in the corn field just where they laid and rolled them in and covered them over with earth. It was a very disagreeable undertaking.

While the Confederates were in town, father had General Stuart to breakfast. After the meal was over, the General stood on the porch in the rain with uncovered head, viewing his troops as they passed down the National Pike. Father got a umbrella and attempted to protect the General from the rain. He pushed it aside, saying that he would not be seen with that over him when his men were marching through the rain.[30]

As the shadows of evening fell, and the guns grew cool, moans and groans could be heard from the farms, barns, and homes in and around Funkstown. These were the anguished cries of the wounded rising in the "evening dews and damps." At the Chaney house, Mrs. Chaney, along with Mrs. Keller, Mrs. Bierly and others, ministered to the wounded. The wounded were stretched out on the floor of the spacious house. Soon there was a pile of amputated limbs in the Chaney yard. One soldier asked a young girl to repeat the prayer his mother taught him, "Now I lay me down to sleep . . ."[31]

Simon Knode watched as dead soldiers were piled into wagons, like cords of wood, waiting to be transported to the Funkstown Cemetery. The smell of gunpowder hung heavy in the night air. Then a light rain began, and a young girl who had assisted in the treatment of the wounded sat down and wept over the sights and sounds she had experienced on this July day, a day she would never forget.[32]

Before darkness, there were other sounds, the sounds of shovels and picks. People in Funkstown, and the farmers, were digging graves to bury the young soldiers from the South, who had fallen far from home and loved ones, never again to receive hugs and caresses of loved ones, and the warmth of the family circle. They had fallen in the cavalry action at Funkstown, Maryland. Later, the dead were moved to the Washington Confederate Cemetery in Hagerstown.[33]

More than four hundred men were killed or wounded at Funkstown, including on the Union side, the Vermont Brigade sustained 97 casualties, while Buford suffered a loss of 99. The Confederates lost 183. More than half of these were in Stuart's Cavalry.

After the cavalry engagement, Meade's infantry paralleled the Confederate position. The Union right flank rested on the Antietam Creek, across the National Pike which went through Funkstown, and thence southwesterly to Jones's Crossroads. The I Corps held the right flank, joined in line by Howard's XI Corps, then the II, III, XI, with Buford's cavalry eventually covering the flank of the XII Corps at Grime's Mill. Kilpatrick covered the Union right flank. After assuming their positions, the Union troops began to entrench.

The troopers of the I Union Cavalry Division, that saved the first day at Gettysburg, were engaged in continuous skirmishing from July 5–13. The men belonged to these cavalry units:

First Brigade, Colonel William Gamble
    Eight Illinois, Major John L. Beveridge
    Twelfth Illinois, (4 companies) and
    Third Indiana, (6 companies), Colonel George H. Chapman
    Eighth New York, Lieutenant Colonel William L. Markell

Second Brigade
    Sixth New York, Major William E. Beardsley
    Ninth New York, Colonel William Sackett
    Seventeenth Pennsylvania, Colonel J. H. Kellogg
    Third West Virginia, (2 companies), Captain Seymour B. Conger

The troopers of the First Cavalry Division, USA, were led by the dependable John Buford, one of the best Union generals. Born in Woodford County, Kentucky, in 1826, Buford was appointed to West Point from Illinois. He graduated in 1848, and saw service against the Indians in Utah and on the frontier. At the beginning of the war, Buford was assigned staff duty and served with John Pope. His abilities were soon noticed by superiors and on July 27, 1863, Buford was promoted to brigadier general.

His actions from the middle of June 1863 to mid July may be unparalleled in the annals of the U.S. Cavalry. Prior to the action at Gettysburg, he was on constant patrol, covering the South Mountain passes, keeping an eye on the Confederates. Buford had "discernment, energy, courage, and skill."

The famous military historian, the Comte de Paris, states that no one can read the accounts of the Gettysburg Campaign, or for that matter the Civil War, without giving Buford and his cavalry the highest praise for the first day at Gettysburg, and also throughout the campaign. Many scholars feel that it was Buford, taking his stand on McPherson's Ridge and surveying the countryside, and making the decision to fight a holding action until the nearby infantry arrived, that selected the battlefield of Gettysburg. Buford's inspiration decided the fate of the battle and perhaps the fate of the nation. Fittingly, a large statue stands in his honor just west of Gettysburg along the Chambersburg Pike.

After pursuing Lee, and being involved in military operations in central Virginia, Buford took sick leave in November 1863. He was exhausted. Sadly, he died at the young age of thirty-seven years in Washington, one "of the bravest and brightest." His commission as major general reached him on his deathbed. The nation mourned, "the loyal and gifted Buford, the man who selected the battlefield of Gettysburg where the two armies measured their strength." President Lincoln attended his funeral.[34]

Buford almost met death on the roads from Gettysburg at Funkstown. In mid afternoon he wanted to obtain a better view of the action.

Shells were exploding in the area, and bullets were whizzing overhead. However, always brave under fire, Buford, accompanied by Abner Hard, the surgeon of the 8th Illinois, walked forward to a slight rise for a better view.

Buford raises his field glasses and scanned the field. He turned and talked to some aides. At that moment, Buford felt a tug at his blouse, almost as though someone had pulled on it. Looking below his right armpit, he saw several holes. A bullet had passed through leaving five small holes. Dr. Hard felt the air of a bullet whipping by his nose. Without a word, Buford, and those with him, retreated to the cover of some large rocks and a clump of trees. The scouting party was over.

Dr. Hard returned to the treatment of the wounded and directed that those who could walk and be transported, be sent back to Boonsboro. There they would join their comrades who had been wounded at Benevola and receive treatment in the Boonsboro Odd Fellow Lodge Hall.[35]*

As a result of the Battle of Funkstown, Meade was now confronting Lee with a line reaching southward just east or along the Hagerstown-Sharpsburg Pike, now Maryland Route 65, from Hagerstown to the hamlet of Fairplay.

---

* Today, as one travels the Old National Pike, there is little to remind a person of those days in July 1863 when the bugles blew, the horses galloped, guidons fluttered in the breeze, and sabers clashed. At the eastern edge of the village of Funkstown there is a marker.

Confederates after Gettysburg, in order to mask entrenching operations along the Potomac River by General R. E. Lee, Confederate troops, led by General Jeb Stuart engaged Union forces under General John Buford. The day long battle east of the road resulted in 479 casualties. The Chaney home served as a hospital, and the Keller home. Major H. D. McDaniel, later governor of Georgia, survived wounds.

—8—

$\mathfrak{Saturday, July}$ 11, 1863

It had been a week since Robert E. Lee had withdrawn from the fields of Pennsylvania. The Army of Northern Virginia was still north of the swollen Potomac River. The Union army was approaching in strong numbers. Some of the Confederates, such as those in the command of Robert Rodes, had been in Maryland for twenty-six days.

A few miles to the east, George Meade continued to probe, ponder and wait. The Union cavalry kept looking for a weak point in Lee's lines, but were unable to find one. There were several skirmishes, and the wounded of both armies were being treated in Boonsboro and Funkstown.

Meade had his headquarters at Beaver Creek, whether it was in the German farming village or somewhere along the stream, is uncertain. He checked reports and awaited orders from Washington. The I Corps, on Meade's right flank, was ordered to prepare breastworks. Halting in line of battle, the soldiers stacked arms, and then charged the "stake and rider fences of the farmers." In moments, the fences were gone, and mounds of dirt formed a good line.

The men in the ranks waited and wondered what might happen. They were sure of two things. First, Lee was still north of the Potomac River, and if he didn't soon leave Maryland, they would have to attack him. If they could defeat Lee, it might mean the end of the rebellion. On the other hand, if the Army of the Potomac were to be severely repulsed, the victory of Gettysburg would be negated.[1] The Confederates would recap the prestige and political advantages lost in Pennsylvania.

II CORPS—USA

The Union II Corps marched from the Sharpsburg area to St. James School, nearer Williamsport. Folks along the way treated the men in the ranks very kindly. After all, they had saved the Union.

Dr. John Kerfoot, the headmaster at St. James, an old Episcopal School, was a friend of George B. McClellan's so the Union troops were most welcome. A tremendous spring provided water to the campus. The soldiers drank from the cold water, and then washed their clothing. There was no time to heat the water, so cold water and soap were used. The clothing was placed on the end of bayonets to dry. Then came the order to "Fall in." Laundry was grabbed hastily, and many a soldier departed St. James with his blouse flying from his bayonet.[2]

III CORPS—USA

The III Corps tramped from Fox's Gap to Keedysville, stopping in the village at 1:00 p.m. for a four-hour rest. Then they crossed the Hitt or Upper Bridge and marched toward the Hagerstown Pike. Bivouac was made about a mile west of the bridge. About 10:00 p.m. they were to march again. This time it was to a location near Boonsboro. Camp was made in a field of shocked wheat. The soldiers helped themselves to the grain.[3]

VI CORPS—USA

The VI Corps was in and around Funkstown. For some rest and relaxation, many of the soldiers went into the village to talk, drink, and look for pretty girls. Robert Westbrook and some of his companions went swimming in the Antietam Creek, and caught some fish for supper. Later in the day some of the soldiers raided a farmer's hen house. A rooster sounded the alarm. The master came to the hen house, but the soldiers had already departed, a chicken in each hand. The men found the sheaves of wheat made nice bedding. Some of the soldiers in the 11th New Jersey prepared for Sunday services.[4]

Senator Henry Wilson was a friend of the soldiers. In the early days of the war, he often visited the campsites around Washington. On July 11 he was near Funkstown. He visited the 22nd Massachusetts and gave an inspiring speech.

XII CORPS—USA

Henry W. Slocum and the XII Corps moved from Bakersville, north of Sharpsburg, to Fairplay. After a halt, it was on to the Jones's Crossroads, a very important road junction. This would become the left flank of the Army of the Potomac as it moved on Lee's lines. The 6th New York Cavalry and 8th Illinois Cavalry were at Bakersville protecting the Union flank.

UNION

Members of the Twelfth New Hampshire and other Union soldiers felt they had Lee, "that old fox," trapped. The end was in sight. Now was "the time to bag him and go home." They complained that Meade was moving too cautiously.

During the chase to the Potomac, Meade conferred almost every evening with his commanders. The appointment of Alexander A. Humphreys as chief of staff increased harmony among the corps commanders. Humphreys was held in high regard by his peers in the officer corps, especially John Sedgwick.

On the eleventh, Sedgwick proposed leading the XI and VI Corps into Hagerstown, taking the city, and moving westward on the National Pike. This would be done during the night. Then in the morning, the two corps would be in position to assault the right flank of the Army of Northern Virginia. This plan was rejected.

Buford's cavalry was now on the left flank of the Army of the Potomac's battle line. Kilpatrick advanced to the edge of Hagerstown and did not find any Confederates.

CONFEDERATES

Between the Sharpsburg-Hagerstown Pike and the Potomac River, Lee had a very formidable line of defense. The right flank rested by the Potomac near Downsville. James Longstreet held the flank, A. P. Hill was in the center, and Richard S. Ewell and the Second Corps anchored the left flank at Williamsport.

The Confederates had constructed strong defensive works, and were itching for a fight. Let the Yankees come, and they would give them a hot welcome. Inspections of the Confederate line, after the retreat, proved that the Army of the Potomac would have sustained heavy losses in an attack on the Confederate position.

Yet R. S. Ewell says he had never seen R. E. Lee display so much anxiety. The Confederate commander had two major problems: the Potomac River in his rear, and the Army of the Potomac in the front. The Yankees would surely come, and all he could do was hope the river would recede. Ammunition was running low, and there was little possibility of breaking out of the situation on the bank of the Potomac.

While the Confederates watched and waited, Edwin Porter Alexander was busy endeavoring to replace the artillery horses lost at Gettysburg and on the roads to and from Gettysburg.

John Casler and some members of the Stonewall Brigade were assigned to the Pioneers charged with erecting a pontoon bridge at Falling Waters. Lumber was taken from places in Williamsport and sixteen boats constructed in two days.[5] Kettles were borrowed from the women of Williamsport to heat tar to make pitch for the boats. When folks objected, Major Harman, the officer in charge of the project said, "Just charge it to Jeff Davis. Our army is worth more than all your lumber in gold."

Meanwhile George Strong spoke in favor of Meade's strategy, saying the retreat on the roads from Gettysburg was not as rout as the press had originally said. Lee was "showing a firm front at Williamsport and Hagerstown. . . . Meade is at his heels, and another great battle is expected.[6]

—9—
Sunday, July 12, 1863

Meade received a lot of criticism for the delay following the Confederates. Looking at the record, however, we have to say this in Meade's behalf.

First, three days after taking command of the army, he fought a major battle. During the three days of fighting, his army suffered 23,000 casualties or around 25 percent. This alone caused problems in reorganization. We have to remember that the VI Corps of nearly 18,000 men saw limited action, thus making the percentage of losses in the units involved much higher.

Second, the Army of Northern Virginia was still capable of giving battle. Supplies were low, but Meade did not know the condition of the Army of Northern Virginia or what Lee might be planning.

Meade had been in command but fourteen days. He had been constantly engaged in seeking Lee, giving battle, and making marches on difficult roads. *He* was unaware of the strength of the Confederate position on the banks of the Potomac, and he knew the risks involved in the event of a defeat.

A major criticism has been that Meade did not follow directly on the heels of Lee, but took a parallel and longer route. Two of the routes he used were very difficult, especially through Hamburg Pass and High Knob. The weather made the mountain roads very bad. Still, another day was lost at Middletown as the Army of the Potomac halted for food and supply wagons.

Perhaps the biggest criticism is the use of the time from July 8–12. From Middletown to Williamsport is about 25 miles. It would seem that Meade's best opportunity would have been to attack Lee as quickly as possible after July 8. The longer the delay, the greater the opportunity for the Confederates to strengthen their position.

Meade anticipated another battle before Lee crossed the river, and preferred to do so in Maryland. As late as the tenth, he was rejoicing in the fact that Lee had not crossed the river, and was hoping that this might be a sign that God was going to bless him with victory north of the Potomac.

However, he realized that Lee's army was not as demoralized and disorga-nized as pictured in the Northern press.

Meade has been blamed for delay, but Halleck must share some of that blame. On July 9, he was sure that Lee was going to fight north of the river, therefore, Meade, according to Halleck, would want "all your forces in hand." The next day Halleck again stated, "I think it will be best for you to postpone a general battle until you can concentrate all your forces, and get up your reserves and reinforcements. . . . Beware of partial combats, bring up and hurl upon the enemy forces."

The roads to Washington and the north would be open, and the fruits of Gettysburg would vanish, therefore, Meade called a council of war for 8:00 p.m. on July 12.

General Newton, who had replaced John Reynolds as commander of the I Corps, was ill, so General James Wadsworth attended in his place. William Hays was there for the II Corps, and French for the III Corps. Again, Meade must have missed Gibbon and certainly Hancock. Three new men were in attendance instead of the older, more experienced corps commanders. Sykes, Sedgwick, Howard, and Slocum were of course there as were Pleasonton, Warren, and Humphreys.

Meade briefed them of the existing state of affairs, saying he felt Lee had a good position and would fight. Meade also shared the fact he was unfamiliar with the ground, and did not know the strength of Lee's position. However, he said he was in favor of moving ahead, but wanted their opin-ion and approval.

Meade asked his commanders to report on the conditions of their men and asked what information they had on the enemy. He then asked for their response to his idea of a reconnaissance in force. Of the seven corps commanders, only Wadsworth and Howard were in favor. No one can question the courage of either man. Wadsworth was formerly a farmer, and after the episodes with Howard's XI Corps at Chancellorsville and Gettysburg, Meade would have to think twice about committing them. Sedgwick had decided against probing the Confederate rear guard in the mountains near Fairfield, and did not relish a frontal assault, nor did Slocum. Pleasonton and Warren supported Meade, however, they were not infantry commanders, so their advice did not weigh as heavily. The council led Meade to take another look, and so on the morning of the thirteenth he reconnoitered in the rain and mist. Later, in the bitterness that developed, Meade became angry over the timidity of his corps commanders, and Slocum blamed Meade for lack of leadership.

Ted Gerrish had these thoughts on the council of war:

We found the enemy entrenched at Williamsport, Maryland, a beautiful village on the Potomac River. We had at last brought the enemy to a halt, and we were once more facing him. We were all anxious for a battle to be fought, for we knew that if Lee escaped across the river, it meant many long, weary marches and bloody battles for us. A council of war was held, and it was found that many of the corps and division commanders were unwilling to make the attack. The army had sustained a sad loss in the death of General Reynolds, and in the severe wounds received by Generals Hancock and Sickles. In all probability, if they had been in that council of war, the Army of the Potomac would have been hurled upon the position of Lee, and his retreat would have been impossible. When the advance was finally made, we found that the enemy was making a rapid retreat in the direction of the Shenandoah Valley.[1]

Frank Haskell, the noted staff officer of the II Corps, felt that those who would have had little part in the assault of Lee's position supported the attack. The I and XI Corps had suffered heavily at Gettysburg. Most people, although they respected Howard, had little faith in the XI Corps. Pleasonton and the cavalry would not be involved in a frontal assault either. Thus, the commanders who would bear the brunt of the attack did not favor the assault. Haskell felt that Meade would have suffered heavy losses, and that once again the North would smell "the odor of sacrifice."[2]

Charles Wainwright expected to move at daylight this Sabbath day. Instead, marching orders did not come until 9:00 a.m. The orders were then countermanded, so it was afternoon before he and the I Corps Artillery moved. Before leaving, Charles took a nice meal with one of the good people of Beaver Creek. The XI Corps, which was in front of the I Corps, had forced the bridge over the Antietam in the morning. Now it was time for Wainwright to go to Funkstown.[3]

New York newspapers, although being a bit premature, or perhaps psychic, were reporting Lee safely back in Virginia with "bag and baggage, guns, plunder and all."

The Monday morning quarterbacks, hailing George Meade just a few days earlier, were now calling him incapable and outgeneralled.

Abner Hard says this was one of the warmest days of the year. The 8th Illinois was preparing to eat on the ground when a severe thunderstorm came. In a few minutes, tents were washed away and the bivouac area covered with water. The artillery of heaven supplanted the artillery of the armies.[4]

CONFEDERATES

Robert E. Lee stood fast, watching and waiting to see what Meade would do.

It was a sad day for soldier Shotwell. He left the Maryland shore, and "our brave comrades in line of battle in front of Hagerstown—left our immense wagon trains huddled upon the riverside—left all aspirations with which we entered Maryland . . . two weeks ago—and once more took up our march down the well-known 'Valley Road.'"[5] Camp was made at Hopewell Church, symbolically near the graveyard.

The Confederates waited all day for an attack to come. They were ready, but Jed Hotchkiss found extensive preparations at the river. He aided Major Harmon in the construction of a causeway to the southern shore. At 3:00 p.m., the wagons of the Army of Northern Virginia started to cross the swift and swollen river, but to ferry 4,000 wagons was a big job.[6]

North of Hagerstown, Early's division moved to the rear of A. P. Hill. Lee thought a second line of defense was needed.

As Lee consolidated his position on the banks of the Potomac, Jeb Stuart and Major McClellan went to the home of a Southern sympathizer in Hagerstown. At 9:00 p.m., the hostess invited the hungry men to eat. At first Stuart declined, but he had not eaten in twenty-four hours. He ate sparingly. Then the lady asked if he might like a hard-boiled egg.

"Yes," replied Stuart, "I'll take four or five."

After the men ate, McClellan went to the piano and started to play. Soon he was singing, "Jine the Cavalry." General Stuart chimed in.[7]

UNION

By 5:00 p.m., the entire Army of the Potomac had crossed the Antietam Creek and was posted along the Sharpsburg and Hagerstown Pike. The Artillery Reserve was to be posted at Jones's Crossroads.[8]

At midnight, G. K. Warren reported that the Potomac had fallen eighteen inches in the last twenty-four hours. Residents of Harpers Ferry told the general that they believed the Potomac could now be forded at Shepherdstown and Williamsport.[9]

Meade was looking at his maps. Howard had reported the enemy on the Wingert, Hillard, Heyser, and Morler farms north of the National Pike, west of Hagerstown.

That day, Albert Welber and the other Yankee prisoners reached Winchester. They had been on the road a week with little or nothing to eat. They were given some more raw meat and a little flour. In Winchester, old men and elegant ladies watched the blue-clad column of prisoners with great glee. They were happy to see such a bunch of Yankees, especially captured ones.[10]

CIVILIANS

Along with thousands of others, Katherine Hewitt continued to wrestle with her grief. The family of John Reynolds begged her to become a part of their lives. She was so overwhelmed by the death of General Reynolds that Katherine entered a convent in Emmitsburg. She maintained contact with his family until 1868. She then left the convent and vanished.

CAVALRY

Kilpatrick and Custer made dashes against the Confederate positions at the beginning and ending of the roads from Gettysburg. However, in the week between July 4 and the conclusion of the campaign, they were very quiet. Custer was more a man of action, rather than the written words. Hence his official report took the form of a diary.[11]

He noted that the 1st Michigan Cavalry lost 26 men that stormy night on the mountain attacking Ewell's wagon train. On July 5, the Michigan Brigade supported a battery during the engagement at Smithsburg. On the sixth, they participated in the actions at Hagerstown and Williamsport. At the close of the sixth, the 1st and 6th Michigan constituted the rear guard of Kilpatrick's withdrawal from Williamsport, "protecting our guns and holding the enemy in check while the remainder of the command fell back toward Boonsborough." Two days later, Custer engaged Stuart's troops on the left of the National Pike near Boonsborough. Custer notes that on the twelfth, he was engaged in the capture of Hagerstown.

The 9th New York Cavalry was at Bakersville. Near Sharpsburg, they noted the numerous graves of those who had fallen during the Battle of Antietam. The horses were kept saddled as the troopers expected fighting to occur at any minute. They noticed the well-built houses and barns, as well as the numerous outcroppings of the rocks. As a part of war, fences were torn down, making way for easy passage as well as campfires. Wheat and straw were taken from the fields and used for bedding, and as an item to soak up the water on the wet ground. The New York troopers obtained three biscuits for five cents from a nice farm lady. One farmer served 1,500 men. One officer was extremely well fed. His rations for the day consisted of beans, potatoes, bacon, bread, butter, raspberry pie, milk and tea.[12]

—10—
Monday, July 13, 1863

UNION

Union lines were now close to positions occupied by the Confederates. Some of the Yankees, feeling that victory was near, had their bands strike up the music. McHenry Howard and other men in gray heard the music. It added a brighter touch to the gloomy weather. On the other hand, some of the Confederates thought they were being taunted. Howard, a Marylander, was depressed. He realized that very soon the Army of Northern Virginia would be crossing the Potomac and heading back to Virginia, but he was not ready to go. George Meade spoke of his council of war.

> I represented to those generals, so far as I knew it, the situation of affairs. I told them that I had reason to believe, from all I could ascertain, that General Lee's position was a very strong one, and that he was prepared to give battle and defend it if attacked; that it was not in my power, from a want of knowledge of the ground, and from not having had time to make reconnaissances, to indicate any precise mode of attack or any precise point of attack, that, nevertheless, I was in favor of moving forward and attacking the enemy and the consequences; but that I left it to their judgment, and would not do it unless it met with their approval. The opinion of the council was very largely opposed to any attack without further examination. I cannot state positively what each individual vote was without referring to my papers. But I am now under the impression that there were but two officers decidedly in favor of attacking; I think that General Wadsworth and General Howard were the only two in favor of attacking, while the rest were opposed to it.

> In view of this opinion of my subordinate officers I yielded or abstained from ordering an assault, but gave the necessary directions for such an examination of the enemy's position as would enable up to form some judgment as to where he might be attacked with some degree and probability of success.[1]

Meade spent July 13 examining the Confederate position. The day was very rainy and misty, and not much information was obtained; nevertheless, on the night of July 13, Meade directed that the next morning at daylight, the whole army should move forward with a view to attacking the enemy.

This order was duly executed, but during the night of the thirteenth, the enemy had retired across the river . . .

Marsena Patrick was also having his troubles with the curious, and the politicians from Washington. They were getting in the way of the troops. He rode from headquarters to Jones's Crossroads. He reported Sunday to be very hot, with a tremendous thunderstorm, but that day was very rainy. Like many others, he realized Lee was short of supplies, yet strongly entrenched. "I should not be surprised if they cross the River tonight."[2]

Wainwright was reflecting on the council of war. His information came from General Wadsworth, who was very much distressed with the decision. Wadsworth hoped Meade or some officer could infuse the men with the bravery to attack Lee. Young Charles felt the general was to be admired for his views, but he thought nothing of the cost and risks involved. "His only idea seems to be that war means fighting. Yonder are the enemy; pitch in." Wainwright felt Lee's position was too strong and could not be carried with a frontal attack. Then came the rains. The land became so muddy that it was difficult even to walk.[3]

Howard sent one brigade of the XI Corps into Hagerstown as an outpost, and to support the cavalry if necessary. He made some personal reconnaissance, using a Hagerstown Church steeple as a lookout. O. O. Howard reported at 11:30 a.m. that the Confederate left "seems to rest on a detached work one-fourth of a mile north of the National Pike, on the farm of Wingert or Zeller. . . . They appear to be very busy entrenching. Their position is on a ridge and very strong."[4] He then ordered General Schimmelfennig to reconnoiter the Confederate left. This brought an exchange of fire. Howard was convinced that Lee would not give battle, but was seeking to quietly retreat. He then asked permission to make a scout in force about 3:00 a.m. the next morning. Meade replied that orders were coming to make such a probe at 7:00 a.m.[5]

CONFEDERATES

While waiting to cross the swollen Potomac, Ted Barclay of the Liberty Hall Volunteers, a part of the famed Stonewall Brigade, wrote to his loved ones:

> Our army has been in line of battle here for two days awaiting an attack from General Meade who does not seem disposed to hurry himself about it. . . . We are strongly entrenched, our line reaching from above Williamsport around by Hagerstown and joining the river again below Williamsport.

I do not think General Lee will stay here long. He is waiting for the river to fall but he will give the enemy a fight if they desire it. The army is in fine spirits, but dirty, ragged and barefooted. I have had on my clothes for nearly a month, my pants are nearly worn out. . . . The army is in such a bad condition as far as clothes are concerned and our means of transportation are so limited and provisions so far to haul that we are compelled to cross the river.

I feel lonesome sometimes with the few of us who are left. . . . I wish that when you send the clothes you would send me a small Bible. . . . My Testament got wet and is torn all to pieces. I have to borrow one when I want to it.[6]

Robert E. Lee had had enough. Ten days had elapsed since Pickett's charge. He had been fortunate, and it was no use to press his luck. With the passing of each hour, his situation became more dangerous, and Meade increased in strength. It was time to cross the Potomac. From his headquarters, Lee drafted the orders.

FIRST CORPS—CSA

Pete Longstreet had been dismayed by the Gettysburg Campaign, Lee's strategy, and the sacrifice of Pickett's Division. He was anxious to return to Virginia. He received orders "to cross the Potomac after dark." Longstreet's command was to cross first. The batteries were "started back about 5 o'clock."[7] The First Corps had but a single road to travel upon. The trains came to a halt and Longstreet rode to the pontoon bridge in an effort to expedite matters. Staff officers were posted along the route to keep things moving. Fires were lighted to provide direction in the black night. Captain J. H. Manning "with his signal torches lighted us across the bridge."[8]

A river crossing is difficult even in ideal situations. The problems with Lee's crossing were intensified. There was a heavy rainstorm, and the road to the pontoon bridge was flooded with mud and water.[9] One of the Longstreet's wagons carrying the wounded plunged into the river. The wounded were thrown into the swollen Potomac. Some, but not all, were rescued in a few moments. Major John J. Clarke and several captains from the Engineer Corps "applied themselves diligently to the work of repairing the bridge."[10] The task required two hours.

Engineers had also constructed at least six redoubts of earthen embankments to protect the crossing. After the accident at the bridge, Longstreet ordered infantry units to occupy the redoubts, and instructed Porter Alexander to place some batteries in line. Old Pete was fearful of a Union attack. He even rode back to the cavalry outposts to check to see if the blue squadrons were coming. When assured they were not, he ordered the infantry back in line. First Corps did not complete its crossing until 9:00 a.m. the next day.

Augustus Dickert spoke for the thousands who never forgot the rainy night in July:

> An hour after dark we took up the line of march, and from our camp, the river, a distance of one mile or less, beat anything in the way of marching that human nature ever experienced. The dust that had accumulated by the armies passing over on their march to Gettysburg was now a perfect bog, while the horses and vehicles sinking in the soft earth made the road appear bottomless. We could march two or three steps, then halt for a moment of two; then few steps more, and again the few minutes' wait. The men had to keep their hands on the backs of their file leaders to tell when to move and when to halt. The night being so dark and rainy, we could not see farther than "the noses on our face," while at every step we went nearly up to our knees in slush and mud. Men would stand and sleep—would march (if this could be called marching) and sleep. The soldiers could not fall out of ranks for fear of being hopelessly lost, as troops of different corps and divisions would at times be mingled together. Thus we would be for one hour moving the distance of a hundred paces, and any soldier who has ever had to undergo such marching, can well understand its laboriousness. At daybreak we could see in the gloomy twilight our former camp, almost in hollering distance. Just as the sun began to peep up from over the eastern hill, we came in sight of the rude pontoon bridge, lined from one end to the other with hurrying wagons and artillery—the troops at opened ranks on either side. If it had been fatiguing on the troops, what must it have been on the poor horses and mules that had fasted for days and now drawing great trains, with the roads almost bottomless? It was with a mingled feeling of delight and relief that the soldiers reached the Virginia side of the river—but not a murmur or harsh word for our beloved commander—all felt that he had done what was best for our country, and it was more in sorrow and sympathy that we had beheld his bowed head and grief-stricken face as he rode at times past the moving troops.[11]

Longstreet never forgot the night crossing at Falling Waters. Years later he wrote his memoirs, *From Manassas to Appomattox,* that green willow poles were placed at the edge of the pontoon bridges in an effort to prevent the wagon wheels from sinking into the mud. However, the "soil underneath was wet and soggy" due to the long season of rain. After a while the wheels began to sink in.

Longstreet continues by saying:

> General Lee, worn by the strain of the past two weeks, asked me to remain at the bridge and look to the work of the night. And such a night is seldom experienced even in the life of a soldier. The rain fell in showers, sometimes in blinding sheets, during the entire night. . . . The best standing points were ankle deep in mud, and the roads halfway to the knee. . . . The current was swift and surging.[12]

SECOND CORPS—CSA

The commanders in the Second Corps have very little to say about crossing the Potomac. R. S. Ewell had a good road to the ford at Williamsport, however, the river bottom had been chewed up by the intense traffic of ten days. Earlier, other wagons had to be moved to higher ground because of the flooded stage of the river. Therefore, almost every wagon in the Second Corps became stuck on the journey to the ford.

The men of the Second Corps had also begun their movement to the river about dark. Many said the blackness was the worst they had ever experienced. It seemed as though "a river was descending from the skies." There were gullies and ruts, and movement was very slow. Bonfires were lighted on both the northern and southern banks to guide the men across. On the bank there was confusion as no one seemed to be in charge. A trafffic master was needed.

Ewell was concerned about his ammunition getting wet. Somehow, the ferryboat had disappeared. Finally, a quartermaster officer recommended that Ewell's artillery be rerouted to Falling Waters to use the pontoon bridge. This was done, but it caused confusion and loss of time.

W. W. Blackford said the ford was almost impassable. The river was quite wide. The fires cast a strange and eerie pall on the river. The light almost danced off the black water, the metal of the muskets, and the horses' equipment. When it came time for the mules to pull some of the wagons across, they bulked and made a terrible noise. Some wondered if the Yankees could hear them above the rain.[13]

Most accounts say it was midnight before the infantry began crossing. Longstreet used the pontoon bridge at Falling Waters, followed by A. P. Hill's Third Corps, while Ewell and the Second crossed at Williamsport. Ewell's men lost 8,000 pairs of shoes in the crossing. About 4:00 a.m. on the fourteenth, Ewell and his headquarters had made it across, and moved into a woods on the Virginia shore.[14]

John B. Gordon, the distinguished general from Georgia, found the Potomac to be a terrific barrier. "The river was deep and muddy, swollen and swift. We were leaving Pennsylvania and the full granaries that had fed us. . . . We regretted leaving.[15]

Gordon remembered the night as long as he lived. The crossing was a little easier for the tall men. For the shorter soldiers, it was an ordeal and they were teased by their comrades. They had to fight the current and seek to maintain their balance. Meanwhile, the taller men shouted, "Hurry along Johnny, or General Meade will help you across."[16]

John Worsham had water up to his armpits. Some of his comrades stumbled on rocks, went into deeper water, and had to be pulled up. The river swept away shoes, and tugged at tattered clothing.[17]

John Gordon was proud of the fact that the Second Corps was the only unit of either army to ford the Potomac on the road from Gettysburg.

He says, "Fording the Potomac in the dim starlight of that July 13th night, and early morning of the 14th was a spectacular phase of the war so quaint and impressive as to leave itself lastingly daguerreotyped on the memory."[18] Gordon must have forgotten the rain.

Gordon also notes that it was strange that both commanders sought to resign after Gettysburg, Lee because it "was all my fault," and Meade because of the abuse heaped upon him from Washington. Gordon states, "It would have been a fatal mistake to have accepted General Lee's resignation. There was no other man who could have filled his place in confidence, veneration, and love of his army."[19]

The finality of roads from Gettysburg was summarized by Randolph Shotwell, "All is over! or rather are all over; for my words apply either to the Trans-Potomac campaign, or the Trans-Potomac crossing of our army."[20]

McHenry Howard shares his gloom:

And so we turned our backs on Maryland. We will in all probability never set foot on her soil again with arms in our hands. What a change in one month.[21]

Howard stood on the Virginia shore and looked back "to our beloved State." He felt that from now on he would be an exile. As Robert E. Lee crossed into Virginia, he was leaving Maryland soil for the last time. The next summer Jubal Early would cross the Potomac, not Lee.

Robert Rodes describes the night:

My division waded the river just above the aqueduct over the mouth of the Conococheague; the operation was a perilous one. It was very dark, raining and excessively muddy. The men had to wade through the aqueduct, down the steep bank of soft and slippery mud, in which numbers lost their shoes and down in which many fell. The water was cold, deep, and rising; the lights on either side of the river were dim, just affording enough light to mark the places of entrance and exit. The cartridge boxes of the men had to be placed around their necks; some small men had to be carried over by their comrades; the water was up to the armpits of a full-sized man.

All the circumstances attending this crossing combined to make it an affair, not only involving great hardship, but one of great danger to the men, and company officers; but be it said to the honor of these brave fellows, they encountered it not only promptly but actually with cheers and laughter.

We crossed without loss except of some 25,000 or 30,000 rounds of ammunition unavoidably wetted and spoiled. After crossing, I marched a short distance beyond Falling Waters and then bivouacked; and there ended the Pa. campaign.[22]

Jed Hotchkiss noted that the pontoon bridge at Falling Waters looked good. The engineers had repaired the bridge on Sunday. They used lumber from some of the storage sheds at Williamsport, hauling the wood about dark, while the infantry began to move toward the river. "All the men were very weary."[23]

Ewell's Second Corps crossing the swollen Potomac during the night of July 13–14, 1863. Fires on the banks of the river guided the men as they waded in water almost shoulder deep. This occurred at Williamsport.

Major Harman builds a pontoon bridge at Falling Waters, using lumber from demolished Williamsport warehouses which had been hauled downstream.

Armies are always indebted to support troops. On the roads to and the roads from Gettysburg, the armies owed a debt of gratitude to the engineers and the men who constructed the pontoon bridges. Without the pontoon bridges at Edwards Ferry, the Army of the Potomac may not have reached Gettysburg in time to save the nation. Also, without Major Harman and the engineers at Falling Waters, the First and Third Corps of the Army of Northern Virginia may have been trapped.

Earlier, the Virginia shore had been alive with wagons. In the early hours of July 14, the shore was alive with troops. Second Corps headquarters was established at Camp Stephen's, a site occupied by Stonewall Jackson on June 20, 1861. At 4:00 a.m., R. S. Ewell reached the headquarters site.

THIRD CORPS—CSA

A. P. Hill has little to say about the roads from Gettysburg. He does say, "We lay in line of battle from the 7th to the night of the 13th, when I moved my corps in the direction of the position of the bridge at Falling Waters." The Third Corps constituted the rear guard of the Army of Northern Virginia. Hill detached Heth's Division "to repel any advance of the enemy.[24] The division of Anderson crossed without difficulty. Pender's Division was

in the "act of crossing when the enemy made their appearance. A small body of cavalry charged Pettigrew's and Archer's brigades, and were annihilated. Only two were killed; but unfortunately for the service, one of them was the gallant and accomplished Pettigrew."[25]

A. P. Hill was on his way home. He had a lot to think about. His men had done well on the first day at Gettysburg. However, after that, his debut as a corps commander was not very positive. He too had lost many officers and men, including his good friend Dorsey Pender. Hill was not in the best of health. He wondered, "How long can the South continue?"

The cavalrymen fared but little better than the infantry. The main difference was that foot soldiers got soaked to their armpits, while the troopers primarily just their knees.

Johnston Pettigrew

The University of North Carolina

For the troopers bank fires illuminated the scene, the water reached the armpits of the men and was very swift. By the bright lurid light the long line of heads and shoulders and the dim sparkling of their musket barrels could be traced across the watery space, dwindling away almost to a thread before it reached further shore. The passage of the wagon trains was attended with some loss, for the current in some cases swept them down past the ford into deep water. It was curious to watch the behavior of the mules in these teams. As the water rose over their backs they began rearing and springing vertically upward, and as they went deep and deeper the less would be seen of them before they made the spring which would bring the bodies half out of the water; then nothing would be seen but their ears above the water, until by a violent effort the poor brutes would again spring aloft; and indeed after the waters had closed over them, occasionally one would appear in one last plunge high above the surface.

In crossing even on horseback the cavalry got almost as wet as the infantry, and they were worse off afterwards, for they had to sit in wet saddles without the warming exercise which walking gives. Having been greatly exposed to the weather during the ten days of rain following the Battle of Gettysburg and then having to take this cold bath in the middle of the night, I felt the next morning very badly, but kept up until we reached the hospitable home of our friends at the Bower, Mr. Stephen Dandridge and his family. Our camp was pitched at the old place in his park and our pleasant, gay life was resumed, with the lovely daughters and nieces of our host. A shade of sadness hung over our meeting, however, when we thought how many who were with us during our former visit were dead or absent from wounds.[26]

Once again the tents and mounts of Stuart's cavalry were at the Bower, on the banks of the Opequon Creek. The previous autumn the cavalry had enjoyed several fine weeks at the Dandridge home, after Antietam, and prior to Stuart's Chambersburg raid. At that time, there was an air of optimism; now the feeling was different.

During the crossing of the Potomac, General Lee, for one of the few moments in his career, lost his temper. Colonel Venable had given him a report that the crossing was proceeding slowly. Lee gave him a reprimand and an order to speed things up. Retiring to his tent, Lee sent for Venable and invited him to have a glass of buttermilk with him.

Venable then returned to his task, and was up until 3:00 a.m. helping to supervise the troops' movements. After guiding the wagon trains across at Williamsport, Venable rode down to the Falling Waters crossing. He soon fell asleep on the Virginia shore. The rain was falling. A little later, Lee crossed and saw his sleeping staff officer. Dismounting, the General took the oil cloth poncho from around his shoulders and covered the sleeping Venable.

—11—
Tuesday, July 14, 1863

The dawn broke with the promise of a clearing trend. After days of rain, nice weather would be most welcome. At daylight, John Buford's cavalry rode forward from their positions near Downsville. They expected to encounter gunfire, but there was none. The Confederate works were deserted. Thinking it might be a trap and a strategic withdrawal, the troopers proceeded with caution. By 7:30, they were certain the rebels were gone.

The Confederates' Third Corps had begun the action at Gettysburg. Only Henry Heth's men remained as the rear guard on the northern bank of the Potomac. Thinking their own cavalry was in front, the infantry felt secure, stacked arms, and rested. Heth and Johnston Pettigrew saw a column of horsemen approaching. They thought it was their own men, instead, it was Union cavalry. They were within one hundred yards when the Confederate leaders realized they were being attacked. The 1st Tennessee grabbed their weapons and used them as clubs to swing at the mounted troopers. One infantryman grabbed a fence rail and unseated a cavalryman. The 13th Alabama and 14th Tennessee opened fire and inflicted some losses.

John Buford's men had moved to the left flank of the Confederates, while Judson Kilpatrick and George Custer made the frontal assault. They were still looking for glory. They hoped they could surround the Confederate rear guard and take a lot of prisoners. Instead, it was their men who suffered, riding through the deep mud, and receiving Confederate fire.

A gap developed in the Union attacking column. Soon, Major Lawrence Weber and the 6th Michigan Cavalry was virtually alone. Other Union squadrons were not up. Weber was an officer who followed orders to the letter. When the Wolverines came within sight of the Confederates, Weber committed his men, he had but 50 or 60 troopers. Buford's men watched the unfolding action with dismay, feeling the unsupported action was most unwise, and showed poor leadership. Regardless of the leadership, most of the officers of the 6th Michigan would soon be dead or wounded.[1]

Although initially surprised, the Confederates recovered quickly, and occupying the Falling Waters' earthworks, laid down a volume of fire.

"Gallant charge of the Sixth Michigan Cavalry at Falling Waters, Maryland . . ."

Frank Leslie's *Illustrated*, August 1863

Captain Kidd's Michigan cavalry dismounted. There was a thud. A minie ball had gone through his right foot, disabling him. Private Halleck assisted the officer to a log house nearby. Confederate artillery shells began falling; however, because the log house exhibited the green hospital flag it was spared.

A few Confederate flags were captured, as well as prisoners. Buford's 8th Illinois began escorting them and the wounded of both sides back to Boonsboro. The muddy roads made the trip most difficult.[2]

The Confederate loss was small in terms of numbers. Even though an officer should not count any more than an enlisted man, the Army of Northern Virginia lost one of their brightest and best at Falling Waters.

Johnston Pettigrew was wounded in the hand at Gettysburg. Thus, it was difficult for him to control his horse. During the encounter, his horse reared, and threw Pettigrew to the ground. While seeking to free himself from the horses' reins, Union troopers demanded his surrender. Pettigrew refused and attempted to draw his pistol. At that point he was shot in the side. The general also fired, killing his attacker. A North Carolina soldier said that the general was killed by a drunken Federal trooper.[3]

There are several accounts of the incident, but the North Carolina troops were eyewitnesses. The Confederate command was not asleep, as some said. It was under arms and ready to repel any attack. They were surprised by the enemy because Heth was led to believe that his cavalry was on patrol. Heth had placed Pettigrew in charge of the rear guard. The North Carolina account states:

> On the night of the 13th we moved in the direction of our pontoon at Falling Waters. This was the most uncomfortable night I passed during the war; it rained incessantly; the roads were eight or ten inches deep in mud and water.

> My command brought up the rear of the army; we were compelled to halt every half mile; the road was blocked by wagons, artillery, etc., in our front. On one occasion we were detained two hours; as soon as we were halted the men sought the best shelter they could find,—houses, barns, fence corners, and dropped to sleep. This could not be prevented as the night was as dark as Erebus, and the rain fell in torrents. A number of men were thus left behind when the march was resumed. About daybreak quite a body of Confederate cavalry passed my command, going in the opposite direction. We reached the heights bordering on the Potomac, where I was directed to halt until everything had passed.

> Enbankments had been thrown up for artillery on either side of the road. The men lay down and went to sleep. There was an open field in our front half a mile wide, then a body of woods. I received orders to cross the river; Pender's division, under my command, commenced the movement. As I was about to move my division, a squad of cavalry debouched from the

woods in our front and approached my troops. Behind the epaulments mentioned, General Pettigrew and my staff, all mounted, saw them approach. We supposed it was the squad of cavalry that had passed us a few hours before. A United States cavalry flag was displayed. I told one of my staff to arrest the officer in charge of the squad and that I would prefer charges against him for displaying a United States flag. I thought he had had a fight with the Union cavalry and captured a flag, and was flaunting it in our faces, thus running the risk of having his men fired on. About this time the squad had approached within 175 yards of my position, and halted. I heard the officer give the command, "Draw sabers, charge!" They soon passed between the open space separating the epaulments, crying out, "Surrender, you d—— rebels, surrender!" A sergeant passed within a few feet of General Pettigrew and myself. In the melee which occurred, Pettigrew's horse reared and fell; as he was rising from the ground, the Federal sergeant shot him in the groin which proved fatal. The affair was over in less that five minutes; the entire squad was killed, wounded, or captured. My loss was General Pettigrew, and one Tennessee soldier. We now moved towards the river and crossed the pontoon bridge.[4]

The loss of Johnston Pettigrew to the Army of Northern Virginia and the Confederacy "was irreparable." A man the stature of Pettigrew could not be replaced. Three days later at the Boyd home in Bunker Hill, Pettigrew expired.[5]

Lieutenant Colonel James Crowell of the 28th North Carolina commanded the last Confederate troops to leave Maryland. Thus, the soldiers led by Henry Heth fired the first and the last shots in the Gettysburg Campaign.[6]

When the 28th North Carolina reached the Virginia shore, the ropes to the pontoon bridge were cut and the boats and planking drifted down the river. Robert E. Lee uttered a sigh of relief. His army was across the river. The Gettysburg Campaign was over.[7] Jeb Stuart gave Lee a cup of coffee which he drank in silence.

Despite the loss of Pettigrew, there were some bright spots. Lee had lost approximately 500 stragglers, sick and wounded, two pieces of artillery stuck in the mud, and some broken down wagons.[8] "All in all, it was a very clean passage of a swollen river, on a . . . dark stormy night, with a powerful foe tugging at our heals."[9]

On a positive note, Colonel A. L. Long noted that although the Army of Northern Virginia was "depressed by its defeat, it did not lose courage for a moment, nor was its confidence shaken in its great commander."[10]

Back on Virginia soil, Ted Barclay was among the members of the Stonewall Brigade pitching their tents at Camp Stevens. It was the location of the first camp of Jackson's men, once they had left Harpers Ferry in 1861. Things were vastly different now. Two years earlier, there were seventy-three men in the Liberty Hall Volunteers of the 4th Virginia. Only three of that number were present in 1863, with a total of eighteen men answering roll call. Ted asks, "Where are the others? Many faces come up to my view who now lie slumbering beneath the sod awaiting the sound of 'the last trumpet.' . . . Why I have been spared these years of toil and danger whilst many promised to be bright and shining lights have been cut down?"[11]

Ted also related that he had left Hagerstown on the night of July 13, marched all night, and forded the Potomac with water up to his armpits. He was very much concerned that the clothing and underwear requested in previous letters had not arrived.

The action at Falling Waters may never have happened if Kilpatrick had turned toward Hagerstown or Leitersburg on July 5, instead of riding to Boonsboro. He noted that at daylight on July 14, his columns reached the crest of a hill occupied by the Confederates an hour earlier. This was at Williamsport.[12]

Learning from the residents that Lee had indeed retreated, Kilpatrick rode rapidly across the muddy countryside toward Falling Waters. En route, he supposedly captured many guns and prisoners. A mile and a half from Falling Waters, he found the Confederates drawn up in line of battle on the crest of a hill. The position commanded the road upon which Kilpatrick was advancing. The Confederates were not expecting an attack. Their arms were stacked.

The 6th Michigan made the attack. "This charge, led by Major Weber, was the most gallant ever made. At a trot he passed up the hill, received fire from the whole line, and at the next moment rode through and over the earthworks; passed to the right, sabering rebels along the entire line, and returned with a loss of thirty men."[13] Alas, Major Weber was among the fallen. Kilpatrick reports a loss of 29 killed, 36 wounded, and 40 missing. He says he found upon the field 125 dead rebels, and took fifty wounded as prisoners.[14]

Captain Kidd called it "the charge of the dare devils."[15] The young officer ordered his men to dismount. As the troopers advanced on foot, Captain Kidd felt a terrible thud. He looked at his boot, and discovered a minie ball had entered his foot. He could not stand. The foot was useless.

Private Halleck helped him to a log house approximately 500 yards to the rear. Shots were flying as the trooper dragged the officer across the open space. Kidd thought the end had come. Artillery shells were also coming and falling close to the log house, even though a green hospital flag was flying.

At 8:00 a.m. Oliver O. Howard sent a dispatch to General Meade's headquarters, saying "no enemy on the Williamsport Road . . . Commenced moving at dusk. . . ."[16] A native reported that there was just one Confederate division left north of the Potomac. That of course was Henry Heth's. Alfred Pleasanton reported at 9:15 a.m. that the enemy was gone. At 10:00 a.m.,

Meade ordered the Second Corps forward, hoping to inflict damage on Lee before he got across. But it was too late.

Soon the Army of the Potomac was moving forward in one of the grandest sights of the Civil War. The line was long, from Hagerstown to Fairplay between Hagerstown and Sharpsburg.

No one who witnessed the advance of the Army of the Potomac to Williamsport will ever forget the sight. The army moved in battle array, "each corps in line, each brigade in columns of regimental front . . . marching over open cultivated fields. The whole line could be seen with its colors proudly floating in the breeze and bayonets by the tens of thousands gleaming in the sunlight. The artillery moved along two parallel roads, in the centre of the mass, all ready for action, while one hundred pioneers from each division moved to the front and swept away obstructions: fences, stone walls, outhouses, everything but dwellings. . . . and large barns. The fields were groaning with the yellow-ripened grain, and when the army had passed everything bore the appearance of having a tornado pass over it. Hardly a stalk of grain was left standing in the fields."[17]

The sight encouraged the men. However, when they found the enemy had gone, their feelings fell. Some blamed everything on poor leadership, but took consolation in the fact that they had answered the call to duty and had done what was asked of them.

In the meantime, the farmers from the Sharpsburg Pike through Downsville to Williamsport would have to face the winter minus much of their crops.

Francis Parker of Massachusetts writes:

Perhaps the finest thing that the army ever saw was the movement forward in line of battle near Williamsport and Hagerstown. As far as the eye could reach on either hand were broad open fields of grain with here and there little woods, the ground being undulating but not broken, and we were formed in close column of division by brigade, the 3d Corps touching our left and the 6th Corps our right; and so we advanced across the wide, yellow fields in two dense lines which extended apparently to the horizon.[18]

Oliver Norton, a member of the V Corps, recorded his impressions:

It was one of the greatest sights ever seen. The whole Army of the Potomac advanced two miles in the line of battle, column by column, ten lines deep. As far as the eye could reach through fields of wheat, corn, and clover that grand line was moving on.[19]

The troops of the Army of the Potomac had ambivalent feelings. Some felt Meade should have been more aggressive, and he had permitted Lee to escape to fight again with more death and dying. Others were glad they had not made an attack. This was after they saw the strength of Lee's lines. Still, others lamented the loss of Reynolds, Hancock and Sickles to death and wounds. These leaders would not have permitted Lee to escape.[20]

I CORPS—USA

Charles Wainwright felt that Meade had used good judgment. He realized Meade would be taken to task by leaders in Washington and also the press. However, in his mind, Meade had done the right thing and had acted wisely. Wainwright said, "Their line of works . . . were by far the strongest I have yet seen . . . built as if they were meant to withstand a month's siege. The parapet was a good six feet on top."

Members of the Iron Brigade passed through the entrenchments vacated by Lee's army. "A glance showed what a slaughter an assault, upon . . . Lee's line naturally defensive line, doubly strengthened by skill."[21]

> Everything indicated a sudden departure. The air was thick with putrid odors. . . . The puffed distended body and legs of a defunct mule or horse dotted the field here and there.[22]

Standing pathetically by the roadside were unharnessed, spareribbed animals. They had served their masters and the army. They were now broken down and of no further use. It was almost as if the animals were waiting to be put out of their misery.

Marsena Patrick said, "Their lines were strongly entrenched—too strongly to be forced by us—we could not attack them safely. . . . The day had been intensely hot."[23]

II CORPS—USA

Thomas Livermore echoed the sentiments of other officers and men. "The Confederate breastworks . . . were well situated at the top of an excellent slope for defensive purposes."[24] Livermore, however, felt they could have been carried.

Robert Stewart was in the Union line of battle, expecting at any moment to receive volleys of fire from the Confederate lines. "To their great surprise and great relief . . . we found them almost deserted."[25] Stewart and other members of the 140th regiment then gathered Confederate stragglers.

George Bruce of the 20th Massachusetts felt that Meade's march assured the Union that the Army of the Potomac was "interposed between the enemy and the capital." As the II Corps reached the Potomac, Bruce noted, "The marches had been hard, but there was no complaining, for the great victory had inspired the men and made them feel that the end of the war was no longer doubtful and nearer at hand." Bruce felt Meade and the army had done well to mass so quickly near Hagerstown and Williamsport."[26]

Brian Bennett of the 140th New York writes that the Army of the Potomac deployed in line of battle at 8 o'clock, "with skirmishers three quarters of a mile in advance. The open ground gave the men a panoramic view of the advance. It was a grand sight to see the columns of infantry as they advanced through meadows and wheat fields with bayonets glistening in the sun."[27]

At 11:30 a.m. from the headquarters of the Army of the Potomac, John Sedgwick noted, "appearances indicate that the enemy has crossed the river into Virginia." Sedgwick then inspected a portion of Lee's line of defense and was impressed with what the Confederates had done.

Thomas Hyde of the VI Corps, as provost marshal, had to care for 1,000 Confederate prisoners of war. They placed them in a beautiful field near the Potomac River. Realizing they were within range of Confederates across the river, and fearing an attempt to free the prisoners, Hyde was ordered to move them to a more secure area.

Meanwhile in Washington, Mr. Lincoln was frustrated. "Our army held them in the hollow of their hand and they would not close it."[28]

In evaluating roads from Gettysburg, many factors have to be explored. For instance, as the 37th Massachusetts reached the Potomac, one-third of the regiment was without shoes. They would not receive shoes or fresh clothing until they reached Berlin.

Alanson Haines marveled at Lee's escape. "The men of the North . . . the Army of the Potomac had stood firm against the enemy, gaining new self confidence and the admiration of the nation . . . (stopping) Lee's great venture, and dashed cold water on the hopes of foreign intervention." The action brought new hope for a united nation.[29] Edwin Bryant of the 3rd Wisconsin felt that had the Union infantry been two hours earlier they could have wrecked Lee's army.

As the Gettysburg Campaign ended, E. P. Alexander and Joshua Chamberlain had their thoughts. Alexander felt that Meade should have struck the Confederate lines with everything he had. That may have been because Alexander knew the strength of the line, and the losses Meade would have incurred. "He could have ended the war at Falling Waters." Gettysburg, Vicksburg, and Falling Waters could have finished the Confederacy.

Chamberlain, on the other hand, felt with many others that the last great battle had been fought. They thought that Lee's army had been seriously crippled. Chamberlain wrote to his wife, "This war, I suppose you can see, is rapidly coming to a close issue, and the heavy fighting is nearly over." Alas, he was wrong. There were miles and miles to go, and battles and skirmishes to be fought. There would be more death and dying, horrible wounds, and broken families. There was still a long, long road to peace.

There was another moment that Chamberlain never forgot. . . . As the V Corps advanced toward the Potomac River, with the skirmishers out in front, tramping through the fields of golden grain, "behind them came the army in full battle array, each corps in line, each brigade in columns of regimental front, with colors flashing in the breeze and the gleaming of sunlight on thousands of rifle barrels. It was one of those rare moments when a man could be deluded into thinking that war is wonderful or at least wonderful until the killing begins. . . ."[30]

Late in the day, marching orders came down from headquarters. On the fifteenth, the various corps were to execute these commands:

The II and XII Corps were to move via Downsville, Bakersville, Mercersville, Sharpsburg, the Antietam Iron Works, and the River Road, encamping in Pleasant Valley, near Harpers Ferry.

The III order was ordered to move via Fairplay, Tilghmanton, to Sharpsburg to Brownsville and camp.

The I and V Corps were ordered to move on the Boonsboro-Williamsport Road to Jones's Crossroads, thence to Keedysville via the Upper Bridge to Fox's Gap. Once across the mountain, these commands would proceed to Burkettsville and Berlin.

The VI and XI Corps were ordered to move by Funkstown on the National Road, across Turner's Gap to Middletown, and then continue to Petersville and Berlin. The Reserve Artillery would take the same route. Meade expected his headquarters to be in Berlin by the evening of July 15.[31]

George G. Meade expressed his feelings, "I start tomorrow to run another race with Lee."[32]

At 3:00 p.m., G. K. Warren of Meade's staff sent a message to the War Department in Washington: "The Maryland Campaign is ended. Have sent to me . . . all the maps you can spare of the Shenandoah Valley and the routes east of the mountains to Gordonsville."

CIVILIANS

The troopers were gone as they had completed their steps on the roads from Gettysburg. They left behind the carnage and desolation of war. Elder Daniel P. Saylor had lived in Illinois and was a friend of President Lincoln. The White House door was always open for the Church of the Brethren preacher. In July, Elder Saylor began a preaching tour of Washington County, starting from his home on the banks of Pipe Creek, Detour, Maryland. He rode to Frederick and then took the National Road westward. Things were fairly normal until he reached the village of Bolivar, on the eastern slopes of South Mountain. O. O. Howard had spent two days on the farms prior to crossing the mountain, and as a result, "the fields were laid waste and all . . . was trampled underfoot." From Bolivar to Williamsport, the scene was the same, "an unbroken scene of desolation and waste. . . . The fences were no more." They had been consumed for campfires, boiling coffee, and easier passage. The golden shocks of wheat were gone, fed to the hungry horses of the artillery and cavalry. Some cattle and hogs were missing, gone to feed hungry soldiers. There was little to note that "these had once been farms." Saylor urged all Church of the Brethren congregations to "turn to the Prince of Peace."[33]

Statistics tell a lot of stories, but the desolation was personal. Samuel Emmerts of Beaver Creek had lost 2,000 bushels of wheat, 28 head of cattle and eight horses. His loss was estimated at $5,000. J. S. Reichard, living near Funkstown, had lost seventeen ham shoulders from his smokehouse. These were taken by the Confederates.

It was a long painful night for Captain James Kidd of the 6th Michigan. He had been part of the attack made by the glory hunters, Kilpatrick and Custer. Some called it the charge "of the dare devils." The two officers spared neither man nor beast.

Private Halleck assisted his commander to a nearby log house. Finally, the gunners saw the green hospital flag and ceased firing. Surgeries were performed and several died as result of their grievous wounds. Moans and groans filled the air. Kidd looked at his friends and comrades. He felt so sorry for them. "It seemed hard that so many bright lights of our family should be extinguished."

Finally, Kidd fell asleep. When he awoke, two ladies who had occupied the dwelling, and had gone to the cellar for safety, were treating him. Later in the afternoon ambulances arrived to take the wounded to hospitals in Hagerstown. Along the route, Kidd saw the debris of war, broken down army wagons and caissons, bloated horses, and hastily buried soldiers, some with just a little dirt thrown over them.

Reaching Hagerstown, Sergeant Barnhart of Troop E knocked on the door of a nice brick residence and asked if Captain Kidd could be treated there. Sergeant Barnhart carried the captain inside. Placing him on a sofa, the ladies fed the captain with tea, toast, eggs, and steak. The occupants of the house were a young couple. They had a little girl, approximately six or eight years old, and were soon expecting the arrival of their second child. When Kidd was feeling a little better, he learned that Captain Snyder of the 1st Michigan Cavalry was badly wounded and dying in a nearby house.

The next morning, Mrs. L and her daughter brought cakes and coffee to Captain Kidd. Mr. L brought him some choice cigars. Kidd remained with the "L's" [we wonder who they were] for almost a week. When he was well enough to leave, they refused to take any money. Kidd boarded a train and rode to Washington where he conferred with one of the army's best friends, Senator Henry Wilson of Massachusetts.

These are some of the stories of roads from Gettysburg. These are some of the vibrations that we may sense in "the evening dews and damps," as we contemplate the farmers and townspeople who lived along the route of marching soldiers, rambling artillery caissons, and galloping cavalrymen. These are the stories of the summer of 1863, when the Army of the Potomac and the Army of Northern Virginia tramped the roads from Gettysburg.

Commanders list, and students read, about army or troop strengths. However, comprising the statistics and the number of troops present for duty are individuals from various homes with families and loved ones. They all have their memories of battles and campaigns.

From a spot near Hagerstown, Private Alexander McNeill of the 2nd South Carolina Infantry recorded his thoughts as he tramped the roads from Gettysburg. To his dear wife, Alexander wrote:

> I am thankful to an ever kind and mercifull God that I have again been spared and that I have passed through the severest battle of the war unhurt. I am at a loss to know how any of us are even left to tell the tale. . . . I regret to record the loss of many a gallant brother in arms. The best blood of old Carolina has been shed and that freely in this battle . . .
>
> In my opinion we have made nothing yet by this campaign. We came here with the best army the Confederacy ever carried into the field but thousands of our brave boys have been left upon the enemies' soil and in my opinion our army will never be made of up of such material again. . . . I never was so completely worn down. . . . We are now at a halt but do not know how long we will remain here.
>
> In haste I am as ever
>
> Your loving Husband
>
> Alex Mc Neill[34]

This was written from near Hagerstown on July 7, 1868.

About noon on July 13, Colonel David W. Aiken, of the 7th South Carolina, wrote to his wife:

> Only because it is raining very steadily, my dearest wife, and I can do nothing else, do I now attempt to drop you a few lines. . . . We are resting here behind breastworks, in constant hearing of the enemy's guns. We will not attack them it seems, and they are evidently afraid to attack us. We have been here four days with the Potomac swimming behind us, with our rations cut down to less than half. Men are exhausted, hungry, dirty, ragged & in many instances barefooted. . . .[35] Orders were issued this AM at daylight to rouse our troops & prepare for action as the enemy is about to attack us, but I suppose the rain will prevent this. If they come upon us they will be whipt; if we go upon them, I rather anticipate a rather similar fate. No one can tell what the next few days may reveal here. We are somewhat depressed at the news of the fall of Vicksburg, but I believe it will only make our men fight the harder, & of course whip the enemy easier. . . . By tomorrow night our wagons may be across (the Potomac) & if the enemy does not then attack us, I think, or rather hope, we will take up our line of march for Virg. soil. This would be cheering news to this army. I don't think Genl Lee or anyone else will ever get it back into Maryland again. I never want to try it over certain.[36]

—12—

After Gettysburg

After Gettysburg there were funerals every day, for weeks. When the fighting ceased, the grim task of burying the battlefield dead began. There were those in Gettysburg hospitals or who had traveled in Imboden's wagon train of misery that expired daily. In the era prior to antibiotics, there was little medicine to fight infections.

Some men, particularly Union officers, were shipped home for burial. Such was the case with John Reynolds in Lancaster, Pennsylvania, and Edward Cross in Lancaster, New Hampshire.

Cross, who had a premonition of death, fell at the edge of the Wheatfield and was brought to the hills of northern New Hampshire for burial. The service was held from the old homestead. The casket was draped with a Union flag, and on the colors rested his sword and cap. The village band played funeral dirges. Local citizens remembered him as "a brave soldier, a true friend, and an impulsive and honorable man."[1]

The local paper, *The Coos Republican*, wrote:

> He was a kind friend, a good son and brother, a brave and chivalric soldier. Devoting his life to his country, he yields it up in its prime and passes away while the nations yet convulsed with the throes of rebellion.
>
> He is gone on the mountain
>
> He is lost to the forest;
>
> Like a summer dried fountain
>
> When our need was the sorrest.
>
> He sleeps near the home of his youth, and among the friends of his boyhood and noble manhood.[2]

Tributes like these were repeated often in the North. Distance and war prevented the sons of the South from returning home.

Meanwhile, George G. Meade was confused about the mixed signals he was getting. He had saved the Union, fought a major battle, and defeated the enemy and was pressing him toward the Potomac. All this within a few days of taking command of the Army of the Potomac, while on the march. Yet, he had his critics: those who felt he had not done enough and was not moving as rapidly as he should.

Robert E. Lee had other things to think about at Bunker Hill. He had lost over 20,000 officers and men on the fields of Pennsylvania. When he crossed the Potomac River northward, there were fifty-one general officers in the Army of Northern Virginia. Seventeen, or one-third, were gone. Lewis Armistead, William Barksdale, Richard B. Garnett, Paul Semmes, and Johnston Pettigrew had answered the last roll call. Another, Dorsey Pender, was near death in Staunton. Isaac Trimble had lost a leg and was a prisoner of war, as was James Archer. John B. Hood had been severely wounded; Wade Hampton, James Kemper and several others had also been wounded. There was no way of replacing the officer corps. Lee traveled for a while with Johnston Pettigrew from Falling Waters to Bunker Hill. He was filled with grief as he thought of Pettigrew's impending death. Of him, Douglas S. Freeman said, "For none who fought so briefly in the Army of Northern Virginia was there more praise while living or more lament dead."[3]

Perhaps Lee saw the handwriting on the wall. Never again would he be able to mount such an offensive with such great possibilities. He had gone so far on the roads to Gettysburg and had come so close to victory. Now, thousands of officers and men were dead or wounded, and Lee blamed himself. Earlier he had said of Pickett's charge, "It's all my fault." At Bunker Hill he wrote to Jefferson Davis saying that if the president had lost confidence in him, he should look for a replacement. Lee spoke of his health problems; he had suffered a heart attack in the spring of 1863. Perhaps a younger man could do a better job. Lee criticized no one, thanked the president for his assistance, and said he would continue to do all he could for the cause of the Confederacy.[4]

At Bunker Hill, Lee also acted in a compassionate manner for the animals. The horses had been without corn for ten days, so he sent the soldiers out into the fields to look for corn.

The Army of Northern Virginia learned of the fall of Vicksburg. William Pendleton said, "It is time to brace up and call on God for help." For John Esteen Cooke, the Confederacy was beginning "to descend into the valley of defeat and the shadow of death."

George Meade continued to write his wife, describing the events of the days and his feelings:

> My Army (men and animals) is exhausted; it wants rest and reorganization; it has been greatly reduced and weakened by recent operations, and no reinforcements of any practical value have been sent. Yet, in the

face of all these facts, well known to them, I am urged, pushed and spurred to attempting to pursue and destroy an army nearly equal to my own, falling back upon its resources and reinforcements, and increasing its morale daily. This has been the history of all my predecessors, and I was disinclined to take the command, and it is for this reason I would gladly give it up.

I consider the New York riots very formidable and significant. I have always expected the crisis of this revolution to turn on the attempt to execute the conscription act, and at present things look very unfavorable.[5]

Headquarters Army of the Potomac

Berlin, Md., July 18, 1863

I try to send you a few lines every chance I can get, but I find it very difficult to remember when I have written. . . . The army is moving today over the same road I took last fall under McClellan. The Government insists on my pursuing and destroying Lee. The former I can do, but the latter will depend on him as much as on me, for if he keeps out of my way, I can't destroy. Neither can I do if he is reinforced and becomes my superior in numbers, which is by no means improbable, as I see by the papers it is reported a large portion of Bragg's army has been sent to Virginia. The proper policy for the Government would have been to be contented with driving Lee out of Maryland, and not to have advanced till this army was largely reinforced and reorganized, and put on such a footing that its advance was sure to be successful. As, however, I am bound to obey explicit orders, the responsibility of the consequences must and should rest with those who give them. Another great trouble with me is the want of active and energetic subordinate officers, men upon whom I can depend and rely upon taking care of themselves and commands. The loss of Reynolds and Hancock is most serious; their places are not to be supplied. However, with God's help, I will continue to do the best I can.[6]

Like Hooker, Meade generally regarded Halleck's dispatches as notes of censure. Both generals had been under intense pressure. Had he received a letter which Lincoln wrote on July 14, Meade in all probability would have resigned. From the Executive Mansion, Mr. Lincoln wrote:

I have been oppressed . . . since the battles at Gettysburg by what appeared to be evidences that . . . (you) were not seeking a collision with the enemy, but were trying to get him across the river without another battle . . .

My dear general, I do not believe you appreciate the magnitude of the misfortune involved in Lee's capture. He was within your easy grasp, and to have closed upon him would, in connection with our other late successes, have ended the war. As it is, the war will be prolonged indefinitely. . . . Your golden opportunity is gone, and I am distressed immeasurably because of it.[7]

However, Mr. Lincoln slept on the letter, cooled off, and never sent the letter; but the damage had been done. Justly or unjustly, the folks in Washington never had much confidence in Meade after the escape. The following year U. S. Grant was brought east to direct the war effort, and in effect serve as commander of the Army of the Potomac.

Meanwhile, back at the Bower on the banks of the Opequon Creek, the clock was turned back—minus many young men. As in the autumn of 1862, Jeb Stuart was singing, accompanied by banjo music. Cavalry head-quarters was located under a large oak tree, called "Stuart's Oak." Saddles and blankets were on the ground and troop guidons fluttered in the warm July breeze. Young troopers and fair damsels walked around the lawn and down by the sparkling stream. They shared conversation and delicious Southern food. John Esteen Cooke wrote, "gay summer nights on the banks of the Opequon! You have flown, but linger still in memory."[8]

Soon the bugles would sound "Boots and Saddles," then it would be time to ride away, never to return. Some say that the gray ghosts of the Confederacy still roam the area, and that if one is still on a quiet summer or autumn evening, he or she might hear laughter, the sounds of the banjo, and the song, "Jine the cavalry."[9]

A. S. Williams had camped in Pleasant Valley near Sandy Hook, in the autumn of 1862, just after the Battle of Antietam. In fact, he chatted with President Lincoln while sitting on a pile of logs. As the XII Corps marched through Pleasant Valley on the roads from Gettysburg, he lamented the damage done to farms and private property: fences gone, fields trampled, and crops destroyed or confiscated. As the XII Corps approached Berlin preparing to recross the Potomac, Williams had a narrow escape. In a letter, dated July 20, the General writes:

> The fields which we left last winter all forlorn and desolate-looking, are now planted all over with corn and grain, but are for the fifth time terribly cut up again, as two or three corps encamped on them and whole acres of wagon trains. I pity the poor people who live where armies encamp. Pleasant Valley has suffered worse than any other spot. This time our visit was especially destructive, as wheat, corn, and potatoes were all standing and as far as the eye could reach were being desolated by horses, herds of cattle, tramping men, and crushing wagon wheels. It is absolutely an impossibility to keep up in the minds of soldiers and employees the least respect for private property. They drive through fields of ripe wheat and over acres of growing corn without one thought of the destruction they are causing.
>
> I sent you from Pleasant Valley a conclusion of our Gettysburg campaign and battle. It was stupidly done, as absolutely I could not get my fatigued mind up to the subject. I forgot also to tell you of a narrow escape I had on the road. I was passing a column of our soldiers and endeavored to take

the side of the road, passing along a deep roadside or ditch on a narrow strip between a stone wall on one side and the deep ditch on the other. I finally came to the end of the wall where a rail fence had been partly thrown down. Here I tried to jump my horse over, but in turning him on the narrow ledge he slipped and tumbling down the bank landed flat on his back in the bottom of the ditch. Fortunately, as he slipped I jumped from the saddle and landed safely on the bank. Old Plug Ugly must have fallen eight to ten feet and as he groaned hugely I supposed he was finished at last. . . . The men got his saddle off while he lay as quiet as a lamb and turning him around, with a big grunt he got to his feet and was led to the upper end of the ditch to terra firma, apparently as sound as ever. . . . Altogether, it was a lucky escape for man, beast, and saddle.

Old Plug was somewhat stiff the next day, but I road him everyday. He is a regular old soldier, however, and takes great advantage of my indulgence and his long service and five or six wounds. As we march along he grabs at every knot of grass, corn, shrub, or any vegetable substance that presents itself on his way. No amount of spurring or whipping can break him of this habit of lying in a supply against short rations. He is an odd, lazy old fellow, sometimes pretending to be very scary, especially after every battle at other times apparently afraid of nothing. For a year and a half we have been daily companions. We get up a great love for even brutes under such circumstances. I should grieve to part with old Plug Ugly, with all his friends.[10]

Gettysburg continued to take its toll. Word came to the Army of Northern Virginia that Dorsey Pender had expired in a hospital in Staunton. He had been struck by a two-inch fragment at Gettysburg. During the long trip with the "train of misery" crossing the Potomac, and the journey to Staunton, his wound became infected, resulting in his demise. Pender's death cast a pall on the army. He had served with distinction and honor. Lee looked upon him as the most promising among the younger officers. Now he was gone.

> They're gone now,
> The Blue,
> The Gray,
> The infantry,
> The troopers,
> and the gunners.
> The wagons, the
> caissons, and
> the cannon have disappeared
> into the mists of time.

But perhaps, just perhaps,
as we travel some of the
old roads, "in the
evening dews and damps,"
We may sense and feel what it
was like in the summer of 1863
on the roads from Gettysburg.

——Epilogue——

MEADE'S REPORT

George G. Meade's report for the Gettysburg Campaign was written on October 1. His report for the roads from Gettysburg is brief:

> On the morning of the 5th, it was ascertained the enemy was in full retreat by the Fairfield and Cashtown roads. The Sixth Corps was immediately sent in pursuit on the Fairfield Roads, and the cavalry on the Cashtown Road and by the Emmitsburg and Monterey Passes.[1]

July 5 and 6 were spent in treating the wounded and burying the dead. On the sixth, John Sedgwick, having pushed the enemy as far as the Fairfield Pass, reported that the enemy held a strong position. They could delay a Union advance "for a considerable time," and Meade, therefore, determined "to follow the enemy by a flank movement." General French, who was in Frederick, was ordered to reoccupy Harpers Ferry as well as Turner's Pass. French had anticipated these orders and sent a detachment to Falling Waters, destroying the pontoon bridge and capturing the guard.

The army concentrated on Middletown, where a halt of one day was made to procure supplies, bringing up the trains to do so. The Army of the Potomac "moved through the South Mountain, and by July 12 was in front of the enemy, who occupied a strong position on the heights of Marsh Run, in advance of Williamsport. In taking this position, several skirmishes and affairs had been had by the cavalry with the enemy, principally by the cavalry and the Eleventh and Sixth Corps."[2]

The thirteenth was spent scouting the enemy position, and preparations were made for the attack. When the cavalry and infantry advanced on the morning of the fourteenth, however, "it was ascertained he had retired the night previous by a bridge at Falling Waters, capturing two guns and numerous prisoners."[3]

LEE'S REPORT

The trains, with such of the wounded as could bear removal, were ordered to Williamsport on July 4, part moving through Cashtown and Greencastle, escorted by General Imboden, and the remainder by the Fairfield Road.

The army retained its position until dark, when it was put in motion for the Potomac by the last-named route.

A heavy rain continued throughout the night, and so much impeded its progress that Ewell's corps, which brought up the rear did not leave Gettysburg until late in the forenoon of the following day. The enemy offered no serious interruption, and, after an arduous march, we arrived at Hagerstown in the afternoon of the 6th and morning of July 7.

The great length of our trains made it difficult to guard them effectually in passing through the mountains, and a number of wagons and ambulances were captured. They succeeded in reaching Williamsport on the 6th, but were unable to cross the Potomac on account of the high stage of water. Here they were attacked by a strong force of cavalry and artillery, which was gallantly repulsed by General Imboden, whose command had been strengthened by several batteries and by two regiments of infantry, which had been detached at Winchester to guard prisoners, and were returning to the army.

While the enemy was being held in check, General Stuart arrived with the cavalry, which had performed valuable service in guarding the flanks of the army during the retrograde movement, and, after a short engagement, drove him from the fields. The rains that had prevailed almost without intermission since our entrance into Maryland, and greatly interfered with out movements, had made the Potomac unfordable, and the pontoon bridge at Falling Waters had been partially destroyed by the enemy. The wounded and prisoners were sent over the river as rapidly as possible in a few ferryboats, while the trains awaited the subsiding of the waters and the construction of a new pontoon bridge.

On July 8, the enemy's cavalry advanced toward Hagerstown, but was repulsed by General Stuart, and pursued as far as Boonsborourgh.

With this exception, nothing but occasional skirmishing occurred until the 12th, when the main body of the enemy arrived. The army then took a position previously selected, covering the Potomac from Williamsport to Falling Waters, where it remained for two days, with the enemy immediately in front, manifesting no disposition to attack, but throwing up intrenchments along his whole line.

By the 13th, the river at Williamsport, though still deep, was fordable, and a good bridge was completed at Falling Waters, new boats having been constructed and some of the old recovered. As further delay would enable the enemy to obtain re-enforcements, and as it was found difficult to procure a sufficient supply of flour for the troops, the working of the mills being interrupted by high water, it was determined to await an attack no longer.[4]

On October 3, Meade reported to General Halleck that his men had buried 126 Confederate officers and 2,764 men before marching on the roads from Gettysburg. This large figure did not include those buried by the soldiers of the XI and XII Corps. The Confederates had also buried a large number of their own dead prior to leaving the field. As Meade departed Gettysburg, there was "a considerable number of dead . . . unburied." Samuel Herbst of Gettysburg had been contracted to inter the dead.[5]

In retrospect, Lieutenant Colonel George B. Davis of the 1st Massachusetts wrote:

> The defeated Confederate army was not destroyed, nor even seriously menaced with destruction, . . . In effecting his withdrawal, General Lee, having an interior line, and reached his objective "by the shortest and most direct routes."

Davis continues by saying:

> There was more wood for fires than food to cook. There was a reasonable amount of forage in the fertile fields past which the armies marched, and altogether too much water.[6]

Water was useful to the armies for cooking and sanitation, but an extra inch or two could make life miserable for troops in the field, and seriously hinder military operations.

The Confederate army was diminished in numbers, but still had adequate force to secure defensive operations. The Army of the Potomac had also been wounded. The I and the XI Corps had suffered heavy losses on July 1. The II Corps helped to save the day on July 2, and received the brunt of Pickett's charge. "In addition, the Army of the Potomac had been pressed closely to its limit of endurance in the long marches" on the roads from Gettysburg.

—Appendix—

A marker on U.S. 11 in Williamsport indicates that Ewell's corps crossed the Potomac on July 13–14, 1863.

Retreating after Gettysburg, the Confederate Army was trapped for seven days by the swollen Potomac River, July 13–14. General Lee with Longstreet's and Hill's Corps crossed here on a pontoon bridge. Ewell's Corps forded the Potomac above Williamsport.

FALLING WATERS' MARKER

Along the Chesapeake and Ohio Towpath.

Retreating after Gettysburg, the Confederate Army was trapped for seven days by the swollen Potomac River. July 13th–14th, Gen. Lee with Longstreet's and Hill's Corps crossed here on a pontoon bridge. Ewell's Corps forded the Potomac above Williamsport.

BUFORD'S CAVALRY—USA

July 1	Holding the line west of Gettysburg.
July 2	Holding the left flank of the Union line.
July 3	Rode to Westminster to guard the trains.
July 4	Riding to Frederick, en route to Williamsport.
July 5	In Frederick all day, refitting, drawing supplies.
July 6	Rode via the National Road at 4:00 a.m. Objective: Williamsport, and the destruction of the enemy's trains. Heavy engagement within a half mile of the trains. Kilpatrick engaged in Hagerstown.
July 7	The division moved to Boonsboro, west of town.
July 8	Battle of Boonsboro. Action began at 5 a.m. Battle lasted twelve hours. The enemy was driven four miles.
July 9	Battle of Benevola. Buford attacked at 4 p.m. Drove him (the enemy) handsomely about two miles.

July 10	Battle of Funkstown. Attacked the Confederates at 8 a.m. and drove him through Funkstown to his intrenchments beyond Antietam when he came out with heavy force of infantry and artillery and gave battle. The division held the crest on our side of the town until its ammunition was exhausted.
July 11	The First and Second Brigades moved in the afternoon to the vicinity of Bakersville.
July 12–13	Remained at Bakersville, and pushed pickets to within 800 yards of the enemy's intrenchments at Downsville.
July 14	At 7:00 a.m. the division was ordered to advance. At 7:30 it was discovered that the enemy had evacuated during the night. . . . The enemy's bridge was protected by over a dozen guns in position and sharpshooters on the Virginia side. As our troops neared the bridge, the enemy cut the Maryland side loose, and the bridge swung to the Virginia side.
July 15	The division moved to Berlin [now Brunswick].
July 16	Moved to Petersville.
July 17	Remained at Petersville.
July 18	Crossed the Potomac River during the afternoon and camped at Purcellville.

I CORPS—USA

July 6	Emmitsburg
7	To Hamburg Pass
8	To Turner's Gap
10	Boonsboro - Beaver Creek Area
12	To Funkstown
14	Williamsport
15	To Rohrersville
16	Berlin [now Brunswick]
18	Waterford, Virginia

II CORPS—USA

July 5	Two Taverns
7	To Taneytown (via 194 and 26)
8	To Frederick
9	To Rohrersville
10	Tilghmanton - Jones's Crossroads Area
11	Jones's Crossroads
15	To Berlin
18	Hillsborough, Virginia

III CORPS—USA

July 7   Thurmont
     8   From Thurmont to 3 miles SW of Frederick
     9   To Fox's Gap
    10   To Antietam Creek
    14   Jones's Crossroads
    15   Burnside Bridge
    16   Pleasant Valley and Sandy Hook
    17   Crossed the River at Harpers Ferry, West Virginia

V CORPS—USA

July 5   Marsh Run
     6   To Moritz Crossroads
     7   To Emmitsburg and thence to Utica
     8   To Middletown
     9   Crossed the Mountain at Fox's Gap
    10   Delaware Mills on the Antietam
    14   Roxbury Mills
    15   To Burkittsville
    16   Via Petersville to Berlin
    17   Crossed the Potomac to Lovettsville, Virginia

VI CORPS—USA

July 5   To Fairfield
     6   To Emmitsburg
     7   To a point near Hamburg Pass
     8   To Middletown and Boonsboro
     9   Beaver Creek
    12   Funkstown
    13   Hagerstown
    14   Williamsport
    15   To Boonsboro
    16   Berlin
    19   From Berlin to Wheatland, Virginia

XI CORPS—USA

July 5   Rock Creek
     6   To Emmitsburg
     7   To Middletown
     8   Turner's Gap
    10   To Beaver Creek

July 12   Funkstown
    14   Williamsport
    15   To Middletown
    16   To Jefferson and Berlin, Maryland

XII CORPS—USA

July 5   Littlestown
    7   To Walkersville
    8   To Jefferson
    9   To Rohrersville
    10   To Bakersville
    11   Jones's Crossroads and Fairplay
    14   Falling Waters
    15   Fairplay to Sandy Hook
    16   Sandy Hook to Berlin
    19   To Hillsborough, Virginia

Notes

INTRODUCTION

1. William M. Owen, *In Camp and Battle with the Washington Artillery of New Orleans*, Boston 1895, p. 256.
2. Jedediah Hotchkiss Journal, July 3, 1863. Mss at the Library of Congress.

CHAPTER 1
"THE GLORIOUS FOURTH"

1. John Imboden, "The Confederate Retreat," *Battles and Leaders of the Civil War* (New York 1884–1887), vol. 3, pp. 420–23.
2. Idem.
3. Unidentified source.
4. Hotchkiss Journal, July 4, 1863.
5. David S. Sparks, *Inside Mr. Lincoln's Army: The Diary of General Marsena Patrick, Provost Marshal General, Army of the Potomac* (New York, 1964), p. 268.
6. *Official Records, War of the Rebellion* (Washington, D.C., 1880–1901), vol. 27, pt. 1, pp. 22–24. Cited hereafter as *O.R.* There are three parts on Gettysburg. Part I is basically Union; Part II is Confederate; and Part III is Correspondence.
7. Sparks, p. 268.
8. Rufus Dawes, *Service with the Sixth Wisconsin* (Marietta, Ohio, 1890), pp. 159–60.
9. Idem.
10. Oliver Willcox Norton, *Army Letters 1861–1865* (Chicago, 1903), p. 162.
11. William H. Powell, *History of the Fifth Army Corps* (New York, 1896), p. 554.
12. Alanson A. Haines, *History of the Fifteenth Regiment, New Jersey Volunteers* (New York, 1883), p. 94.
13. Idem.
14. Alfred S. Roe, *The Tenth Regiment Massachusetts Volunteer Infantry, 1861–1864* (Springfield, 1909), p. 210. This feeling was expressed by many as they were grateful for their survival, but lamented the loss of comrades.
15. George K. Collins, *Memoirs of the 149th Volunteers Infantry* (Syracuse, 1891), p. 147.

16. Douglas S. Freeman, *Robert E. Lee* (New York, 1935), vol. 3, p. 135.

17. James Longstreet, *From Manassas to Appomattox* (Philadelphia, 1896), p. 428. Attributed to James Longstreet.

18. Quoted in one of the dispatches of Charles C. Coffin writing for his Boston paper.

19. Hotchkiss Journal, July 4, 1863.

20. Andrew Curtin Papers in the John F. Reynolds Papers, Lancaster, Pa.

21. Edward J. Nichols, *Toward Gettysburg* (State College, Pa., 1958), p. 212.

22. Luther W. Hopkins, *From Bull Run to Appomattox, A Boy's View* (Baltimore, n.d.), p. 160.

23. *O.R.,* pt. 2, p. 699.

24. James A. L. Fremantle, *Three Months in the Southern States, April–June 1863* (New York, 1864), pp. 22, 218–19.

25. Imboden, pp. 422–23.

26. *O.R.,* pt. 2, pp. 309, 311.

27. Ibid., p. 448.

28. Hopkins, p. 105.

29. Idem.

30. *O.R.,* pt. 1, p. 998.

31. *O.R.,* pt. 1, p. 928.

32. Idem.

CHAPTER 2
A RAINY SUNDAY

1. Walter Clark, ed., *Histories of Several Regiments and Battalions from North Carolina in the Great War, 1861–1865* (Raleigh, 1902) vol. 1, p. 181. Cited hereafter as Clark.

2. Jacob Hoke, *The Great Invasion* (Dayton, 1887), p. 478.

3. Ibid., p. 500.

4. Ibid., p. 501.

5. Ibid., p. 506.

6. Imboden, p. 422.

7. Interview with Mr. Victor Birely, a distinguished Civil War and Lincoln scholar. The account was passed down through the family.

8. *O.R.,* pt. 2, p. 700.

9. Ibid., pp. 992–93.

10. Roger Keller, *Events of the Civil War in Washington County, Maryland* (Shippensburg, Pa., 1995), pp. 152–53.

11. *O.R.,* pt. 2, p. 700.

12. Ibid., pp. 470–72.

13. Fremantle, pp. 222–24.

14. Freeman, vol. 3, p. 135.

15. Harry Gilmor, *Four Years in the Saddle* (New York, 1866), pp. 233–34.

16. J. W. Polk, *The North and South American Review* (C. Austin, 1912), p. 26.

17. Arthur Crew, ed., *Soldier of the South: General Pickett's War Letter to His Wife* (Boston, 1928), pp. 100–2.

18. Augustus Dickert, *A History of Kershaw's Brigade* (New Berry, S.C., 1899), pp. 285–86.

19. Fremantle, pp. 222–24.

20. *O.R.,* pt. 2, p. 448.

21. Ibid., p. 534.

22. Ibid., p. 635.

23. Freemantle, pp. 222–24.
24. *O.R.,* pt. 2, p. 496.
25. Ibid., p. 322.
26. Imboden, p. 42.
27. Alan Nevins, ed., *A Diary of Battle: The Personal Journal of Colonel Charles S. Wainwright, 1861–1865* (New York, 1962), July 5, 1863, account. Cited hereafter as Wainwright Journal.
28. Theodore Gerrish, *Army Life: A Private's Reminiscences of the Civil War* (Portland, 1882), p. 272.
29. Haines, p. 96.
30. James L. Bowen, *History of the Thirty-seventh Regiment Massachusetts Volunteers* (Holyoke, Mass., 1884), pp. 191–192.
31. Edmund Brown, *The Twenty-seventh Indiana Infantry Volunteers,* n.p., 1899, p. 427.
32. Sullivan D. Green, Letters from Gettysburg to the *Detroit Free Press,* July 2–5, 1863.
33. Wainwright Journal, July 5, 1863.
34. Thomas Gawley, *The Valiant Hours* (Harrisburg, 1964), p. 14.
35. David Craft, *History of the One Hundred Forty-first Regiment Pennsylvania Volunteers* (Towanda, Pa., 1885), p. 138.
36. Henry Taylor to his parents, Isaac Lynn Taylor Letters, Morrison County, Minn., Historical Society.
37. *Antietam to Appomattox with the One Hundred and Eighteenth Pennsylvania "Volunteers" Corn Exchange Regiment* (Philadelphia, 1892), p. 272.
38. Norton, p. 165.
39. James S. Rusling, *Men and Things I Saw in the Civil War* (New York, 1889), p. 124.
40. Idem.
41. *O.R.,* pt. 3, pp. 530–31.
42. Meade to Halleck, July 5, 1863, *in O.R.*, pt. 3, p. 93.
43. Idem.
44. *O.R.,* pt. 3, July 4, 1863, 4:15 p.m., p. 519.
45. Ibid., p. 533.
46. Meade to his wife, in *The Life and Letters of Major General George Gordon Meade* (New York, 1913), vol. 2, p. 98.
47. Harry M. Kieffer, *Recollections of a Drummer Boy* (Boston, 1889), p. 89.
48. *The New York Tribune,* July 5, 1863.
49. Washington County Maryland Bicentennial Program, and interview with Mrs. William Young, July 1976.
50. *The New York Tribune,* July 15, 1863.
51. Abner Hard, *History of the Eighth Cavalry Regiment, Illinois Volunteers* (Chicago, Ill., 1888), p. 261.

CHAPTER 3
ARMIES ON THE MOVE

1. Sedgwick to Meade, July 5, 1863.
2. *O.R.,* pt. 2, p. 311.
3. Nelson Hutchinson, *History of the Seventh Regiment Massachusetts Infantry* (Taunton, Mass., 1890), p. 157.
4. Roe, p. 211.
5. Hutchinson, p. 157.

6. Dawes, p. 161.

7. Wainwright Journal, July 6, 1863.

8. Kieffer, p. 90.

9. Patrick, p. 269.

10. Idem.

11. Frank Sawyer, *A Military History of the Eighth Regiment Ohio Infantry* (Cleveland, 1881), p. 135.

12. Collins, p. 47.

13. Henry Taylor writing to his parents, July 6, 1863.

14. Idem.

15. Charles Bardeen, *A Little Fifer's War Diary* (Syracuse, 1910), p. 239.

16. Samuel Toombs, *Reminiscences of the War . . . Experiences of the Thirteenth Regiment, New Jersey Volunteers* (Orange, N.J., 1878), pp. 85–87.

17. Collins, pp. 47, 152.

18. Toombs, pp. 85–87.

19. Joshua Lawrence Chamberlain Papers, Bowdoin College (Brunswick, Me.).

20. Idem.

21. *O.R.,* pt. 2, p. 361.

22. Idem.

23. Fremantle, p. 224.

24. George P. Pickett, to his beloved, July 6, 1863.

25. E. P. Alexander, *Military Memoirs of a Confederate* (New York, 1907), p. 301.

26. Hotchkiss Journal, July 6, 1863.

27. *O.R.,* pt. 2, p. 472.

28. Ted Barclay, of the Liberty Hall Volunteers, writing to his sister on July 8 and July 13, 1863, McCormick Library, Washington-Lee University, Lexington, Va.

29. Imboden, p. 42.

30. *O.R.,* pt. 2, pp. 701–2.

31. Ibid.

32. *Battles and Leaders,* vol. 3, p. 425.

33. *O.R.,* pt. 2, p. 702.

34. *O.R.,* pt. 1, p. 995.

35. *O.R.,* pt. 2, p. 499.

36. The street fighting in Hagerstown was one of the momentous events on the roads from Gettysburg, *O.R.,* pt. 1, p. 935.

37. *O.R.,* pt. 1, p. 995.

38. Harry Gilmor, *Four Years in the Saddle* (New York, 1866), p. 101.

39. *O.R.,* pt. 2, pp. 702–3.

40. Ibid., pp. 436–37.

41. Imboden, p. 422.

42. Idem.

43. *O.R.,* pt. 2, pp. 702–3.

44. Imboden, pp. 425–26.

45. Ibid., p. 428.

46. Worsham, p. 108.

47. *O.R.,* pt. 1, p. 925.

48. Ibid., p. 938.

49. Idem.

50. *O.R.*, pt. 2, p. 581.

51. Longmeadow Church of the Brethren records, and Rowland family papers, Hagerstown, Md.

52. Idem.

CHAPTER 4
TUESDAY, JULY 7, 1863

1. *O.R.*, pt. 3, p. 567.

2. The Honorable Edward S. Delaplaine in a series of articles written for the *Frederick New Post*, July 1973. Judge Delaplaine was a distinguished historian, writing on Francis Scott Key, Roger Brook Taney, John Philip Sousa, and others. His legacy has made it possible for the National Museum of Civil War Medicine to begin operation on East Patrick Street in Frederick, Maryland.

3. George G. Meade to his wife, July 7, 1863.

4. Idem.

5. W. A. Crofut in *St. Paul–Minneapolis Pioneer Press*, December 7, 1884.

6. Orson B. Curtis, *History of the Twenty-fourth Michigan* (Detroit, 1891), p. 46.

7. Charles E. Davis, *The Story of the Thirteenth Massachusetts Volunteers* (Boston, 1894), pp. 250–51.

8. Kieffer, p. 60.

9. Wainwright Journal, July 7, 1863.

10. Bardeen, p. 211.

11. Idem.

12. Craft, p. 141.

13. Hutchinson, p. 218.

14. The student of roads from Gettysburg can still gollow the V Corps on the road from Gettysburg to Frederick, on the Old Frederick Road.

15. Hutchinson, p. 99.

16. Idem.

17. Thomas W. Hyde, *Following the Greek Cross or Memories of the Sixth Army Corps* (Boston, 1894), p. 159.

18. *O.R.*, pt. 2, p. 935.

CHAPTER 5
WEDNESDAY, JULY 8, 1863

1. Meade, *Life and Letters*, vol. 2, p. 180.

2. Ibid., p. 179.

3. Curtis, p. 193.

4. Wainwright Journal, pp. 256–58.

5. Augustus Buell, *The Cannoneer* (Washington, D.C.), p. 122.

6. *O.R.*, pt. 1, p. 296.

7. Livermore, p. 270.

8. Idem.

9. *O.R.*, pt. 1, p. 708.

10. Idem.

11. Idem.
12. Ibid., p. 925.
13. Idem.
14. Idem.
15. Idem.
16. *O.R.,* pt. 2, p. 703.
17. Idem.
18. Idem.
19. Idem.
20. Hotchkiss Journal, July 8, 1863.
21. Idem.
22. Idem.

CHAPTER 6
THURSDAY, JULY 9, 1863

1. Meade, *Life and Letters*, vol. 2, p. 121.
2. Curtis, p. 194.
3. Dawes, p. 154.
4. Wainwright Journal, July 9, 1863, p. 258.
5. Charles Page, *The Fourteenth Connecticut* (Meridian, Conn., 1906), pp. 169–70.
6. Bardeen, p. 242.
7. Craft, p. 135.
8. Houghton, pp. 108–9.
9. Haines, p. 99.
10. *O.R.,* pt. 1, p. 708.
11. Ibid., p. 270.
12. Ibid., p. 271.
13. *O.R.,* pt. 2, p. 703.
14. Ibid., pt. 1, pp. 925–26.
15. Ibid., pp. 940–41.
16. Imboden, p. 429.
17. Shotwell, vol. 2, p. 37.
18. Idem.
19. Moore, p. 155.
20. Imboden, p. 429.

CHAPTER 7
FRIDAY, JULY 10, 1863

1. Meade, *Life and Letters*, vol. 2, p. 179.
2. Ibid., p. 180.
3. Meade to Halleck, July 10, 1863.
4. Idem.
5. Idem.
6. Idem.
7. Idem.
8. Halleck to Meade, July 10, 1863.

9. Wainwright Journal, July 11, 1863, pp. 258–59.

10. Curtis, p. 194.

11. Cudworth, p. 407.

12. Idem.

13. Patrick, p. 270.

14. Idem.

15. The Chamberlain Papers.

16. Hyde, p. 162.

17. Ibid, p. 163.

18. *O.R.,* pt. 1, p. 712.

19. The cavalry battle of Funkstown, just east of the village on July 10, 1863.

20. *O.R.,* pt. 1, p. 712.

21. Ibid., p. 771.

22. Ibid., p. 791.

23. Hotchkiss Journal, July 10, 1863.

24. Fremantle, p. 224.

25. Moore, p. 156.

26. Stuart to his wife, July 10, 1863.

27. *O.R.,* pt. 1, p. 929.

28. Ibid., p. 936.

29. Ibid., pp. 941–42.

30. The Stonebraker name is prominent in Washington County, Maryland. Young Jacob was a Southern sympathizer living in Funkstown and was an eyewitness to the battle. He later had some accounts of the action printed.

31. Interview with William Bierly, known as the Funkstown historian, and a descendant of some of the folks who lived in the village in 1863.

32. Stonebraker accounts.

33. The Washington Confederate Cemetery. The cemetery is located on South Potomac Street in Hagerstown, Md.

34. Edward Longacre, *General John Buford: A Military Biography* (Conshohocken, Pa., 1995), p. 246.

35. Hard, p. 264.

CHAPTER 8
SATURDAY, JULY 11, 1863

1. Wainwright Journal, July 11, 1863, p. 259.

2. Stewart, pp. 145–17.

3. Child, pp. 137–18.

4. Thomas Marbaker, *History of the Eleventh New Jersey Volunteers* (Trenton, 1898), p. 113.

5. John Casler, *Four Years in the Stonewall Brigade* (Marietta, Ga., 1951), pp. 180–81.

CHAPTER 9
SUNDAY, JULY 12, 1863

1. Gerrish, p. 131.

2. Haskell, p. 131.

3. Wainwright Journal, July 12, 1863.

4. Hard, p. 264.

5. Shotwell, vol. 2, p. 37.

6. Hotchkiss Journal, July 12, 1863.

7. H. B. McClellan, *The Life and Campaigns of Major General J.E.B. Stuart* (Boston, 1885), p. 280.

8. *O.R.,* pt. 1, p. 709.

9. Ibid., p. 669.

10. Albert Welber, "From Gettysburg to Libby Prison," The Gettysburg Papers, vol. 1 (Dayton, 1978).

11. *O.R.,* pt. 1, p. 671.

12. Cheney, pp. 120–22.

CHAPTER 10
MONDAY, JULY 13, 1863

1. Meade, *Life and Letters*, vol. 2, p. 13.

2. Patrick, pp. 270–72.

3. Wainwright Journal, July 13, 1863.

4. *O.R.,* pt. 1, p. 708.

5. Idem.

6. Ted Barclay writing to his sister, July 8, 1863.

7. Longstreet, p. 429; and *O.R.,* pt. 3, p. 1,000.

8. *O.R.,* pt. 1, p. 147.

9. *O.R.,* pt. 3, p. 669.

10. Dickert, pp. 258–69.

11. *O.R.,* pt. 1, p. 998.

12. *O.R.,* pt. 2, p. 361.

13. Blackford, p. 234.

14. Hotchkiss Journal, July 14, 1863.

15. Gordon, pp. 172–73.

16. Idem.

17. Worsham, p. 109.

18. Gordon, p. 173.

19. Idem.

20. Shotwell, vol. 2, p. 40.

21. McHenry Howard, *Recollections of a Maryland Staff Officer* (Dayton, 1975), p. 217.

22. *O.R.,* pt. 2, p. 548.

23. Hotchkiss Journal, July 14, 1863.

24. *O.R.,* pt. 2, p. 609.

25. Idem.

26. Blackford, pp. 234–35.

CHAPTER 11
TUESDAY, JULY 14, 1863

1. *O.R.,* pt. 1, p. 929.

2. Ibid., p. 996.

3. Walter Clark, ed., *Histories of the Several Regiments and Battalions from North Carolina in the Great War*, vol. 5 (Raleigh, 1901), p. 101.

4. *O.R.,* pt. 2, p. 555.

5. Clark, ed., vol. 2, pp. 376–77.

6. *O.R.,* pt. 2, p. 609.
7. Cooke, p. 31.
8. Shotwell, vol. 2, p. 41.
9. Idem.
10. Al Long, *Memoirs of Robert E. Lee* (New York, 1886), p. 41.
11. Barclay writing to his sister, July 14, 1863.
12. *O.R.,* pt. 1, p. 985.
13. Idem.
14. Idem.
15. Kidd, p. 183.
16. *O.R.,* pt. 1, p. 709.
17. Powell, p. 567.
18. Francis J. Parker, *The Story of the Thirty-second Massachusetts Infantry* (Boston, 1889), p. 175.
19. Norton, p. 166.
20. Regis De Trobriand, *Four Years in the Army of the Potomac* (Boston, 1889), p. 524.
21. Wainwright Journal, p. 262; and Curtis, p. 194.
22. Curtis, pp. 194–95.
23. Patrick, p. 271.
24. Livermore, p. 272.
25. Stewart, p. 147.
26. Bruce, p. 300.
27. Bennett, p. 236.
28. Lincoln thought Meade should have bagged Lee's army at Williamsport.
29. Haines, p. 100.
30. Chamberlain Papers.
31. *O.R.,* pt. 3, p. 693.
32. Meade, *Life and Letters*, vol. 2, p. 133.
33. D. P. Saylor, "Gospel Visitor," September 1863. Saylor was a friend of Lincoln's and may have baptized him. The original is in the hands of the Ropp family of Linwood, Maryland.
34. Alex McNeill to his wife, July 7, 1863.
35. David W. Aiken to his wife, July 7, 1863.
36. Idem.

CHAPTER 12
AFTER GETTYSBURG

1. *The Coos Republican* (Lancaster, New Hampshire), July 14, 1863.
2. Idem.
3. Freeman, 190.
4. Lee to Davis, July 13, 1863.
5. Meade, *Life and Letters*, vol. 2, p. 134.
6. Ibid., p. 135.
7. Lincoln to Meade, July 14, 1863.
8. John Easteen Cooke, *Mohun or the Last Days of Lee* (Charlottesville, 1936), p. 69.
9. Idem.
10. A. S. Williams to his daughters, July 20, 1863.

EPILOGUE

1. *O.R.,* pt. 1, p. 117.
2. Ibid., p. 118.
3. Idem.
4. *O.R.,* pt. 2, pp. 306–11.
5. *O.R.,* pt. 1, p. 119.
6. George B. Davis in the Gettysburg Papers.

Bibliography

Alexander, E. P. *Military Memoirs of a Confederate*. New York, 1907.

The Ted Barclay Letters, Special Collections Department, the McCormick Library, Washington and Lee University, Lexington, Virginia.

Bardeen, Charles. W. *A Little Fifer's Diary*. Syracuse, 1910.

Barlow, Francis. Papers in the Massachusetts Historical Society.

Bartlett, A. W. History of the Twelfth Regiment New Hampshire Volunteers. Concord, 1897.

Best, Isaac O. *History of the One Hundred Twenty-first New York State Infantry*. Chicago, 1921.

Bicknell, George W. *History of the Fifth Regiment Maine Volunteers*. Portland, 1871.

Blackford, W. W. *War Years With Jeb Stuart*. New York, 1946.

Boies, Andrew. *Record of the Thirty-third Massachusetts Volunteer Infantry*. Firchburg, 1880.

Boudrye, Louis N. *Historic Events of the Fifth New York Cavalry*. Albany, 1864.

Bowen, James L. *History of the Thirty-seventh Regiment Massachusetts Volunteers*. Holyoke, 1884.

Brown, Edmund. *The Twenty-seventh Indiana Volunteer Infantry,* n.p., 1899.

Bryant, Edwin E. *History of the Third Regiment Wisconsin Volunteer Infantry*. Madison, 1891.

Buell, Augustus. *The Cannoneer*. Washington, 1890.

Caldwell, J. F. K. *The History of a Brigade of South Carolinians*. Philadelphia, 1886.

Casler, John. *Four Years in the Stonewall Brigade*. Marietta, Ga., 1951.

Chamber of Commerce. *Encounter At Hanover*. Gettysburg, 1962.

The Joshua Chamberlain Papers, Bowdoin College Brunswick, Maine.

Cheney, Newel. *History of the Ninth Regiment New York Volunteer Cavalry*. Poland Center, N.Y., 1901.

Child, William. *History of the Fifth Regiment New Hampshire Volunteers*. Bristol, 1893.

Clark, Walter, ed. *Histories of the Several Regiments and Battalions from North Carolina in the Great Wars*. Raleigh, 1901.

Coffin, Charles. Accounts in the *Boston Journal* (July 1863).

Collins, George K. *Memoirs of the 149th Regiment New York Volunteer Infantry*. Syracuse, 1891.

Cooke, John Esteen. *Mohun or the Last Days of Lee*. Charlottesville, 1936.

Craft, David. *History of the One Hundred Forty-first Regiment Pennsylvania Volunteers*. Towanda, 1885.

Crotty, D. G. *Four Years Campaigning in the Army of the Potomac*. Grand Rapids, 1874.

Cudworth, Warren H. *History of the First Regiment Massachusetts Infantry*. Boston, 1866.

Curtis, Orson B. *History of the Twenty-fourth Michigan*. Detroit, 1891.

Daffan, Katie. *My Father As I Remember Him*. Houston, 1904.

Davis, Charles. *The Story of the Thirteenth Massachusetts Volunteers*. Boston, 1894.

Dawes, Rufus. *Service with the Sixth Wisconsin Volunteers*. Marietta, Ohio, 1890.

Delaplaine, Edward S. "The Change Of Command." *The Frederick News-Post* (July 1973).

De Trobriand, Regis. *Four Years with the Army of the Potomac*. Boston, 1889.

Dickert, Augustus. *A History of Kershaw's Brigade*. Newberry, S.C., 1899.

Douglas, Henry K. *I Rode With Stonewall*. Chapel Hill, 1940.

Dunge, William H., ed. *Four Years in the Confederate Artillery, a Diary of Private Henry Robison Berkley*. Chapel Hill, 1961.

Engelbrecht, Jacob. *Diary and private papers*. Frederick, Md., 1863.

Freeman, Douglas S. *Lee's Lieutenants*. New York, 1943.

Freeman, Douglas S. *Robert E. Lee*. New York, 1935.

Fremantle, James A. *Three Months in the Southern States, April–June, 1863*. New York, 1864.

Gawley, Thomas. *The Valiant Hours*. Harrisburg, 1964.

Gerrish, Theodore. *Army Life: A Private's Reminiscences of the Civil War*. Portland, 1882.

Gibbon, John. *Personal Recollections of the War*. New York, 1928.

Gildersleeve, Jennie. Letter in the Reynolds Papers. Franklin and Marshall College, Lancaster, Pa.

Gilmor, Harry. *Four Years in the Saddle*. New York, 1886.

Gordon, John. *Reminiscences of the Civil War*. New York, 1904.

Graceham Moravian Church Records. Graceham, Frederick County, Md., 1863.

Hall, Hillman. *History of the Fifteenth Regiment New Jersey Volunteers*. New York, 1883.

Hamilton, James, ed. *The Papers of Randolph Shotwell*. Raleigh, 1929.

Hamlin, Percy. *Old Bald Head*. Strasburg, Va., 1940.

Hard, Abner. *History of the Eighth Cavalry Regiment, Illinois Volunteers*. Chicago, 1888.

Haskell, Frank A. *The Battle of Gettysburg*. Boston, 1969.

Haupt, Herman. *Reminiscences of General Herman Haupt*. Milwaukee, 1901.

Hoke, Jacob. *The Great Invasion*. Dayton, 1887.

Hotchkiss, Jed. Manuscript in the Library of Congress.

Houghton, Edwin B. *The Campaigns of the Seventeenth Maine*. Portland, 1886.

Howard, McHenry. *Recollections of a Maryland Staff Officer*. Dayton, 1975.

Howard, Oliver O. *Autobiography of Oliver O. Howard, Major General*. New York, 1907.

Hyde, Thomas. *Following the Greek Cross or Memories of the Sixth Army Corps*. Boston, 1884.

Imboden, John. "The Confederate Retreat." *Battles and Leaders*. New York, Vol. 3 (1884).

Inman, Arthur Crew. *Soldiers of the South: General Pickett's War Letters to His Wife*. Boston, 1928.

Kidd, J. H. *Personal Recollections of a Cavalryman*. Grand Rapids, 1969.

Kieffer, Harry M. *Recollections of a Drummer Boy*. Boston, 1889.

Klein, Frederick, ed. *Just South of Gettysburg: Carroll County, Maryland in the Civil War*. Lancaster, 1974.

Lee, Susan P. *The Memoirs of Robert E. Lee*. New York, 1886.

Longstreet, James. *From Manassas to Appomattox*. Philadelphia, 1886.

McClellan, H. B. *The Life and Campaigns of Major General J. E. B. Stuart*. Boston, 1885.

McDonald, William N. *A History of the Laurel Brigade, Originally the Ashby Cavalry of the Army of Northern Virginia and Chews Battery*. Baltimore, 1907.

McNamara, Daniel. *The History of the Ninth Regiment, Massachusetts Infantry*. Boston, 1889.

Marbaker, Thomas. *History of the Eleventh New Jersey Volunteers*. Trenton, 1898.

Meade, George, Jr., ed. *The Life and Letters of Major General George Gordon Meade*. New York, 1913.

Murphy, Thomas. *History of the First Regiment Delaware Volunteers*. Philadelphia, 1866.

Nevins, Allan, ed. *A Diary of Battle the Personal Journal of Colonel Charles S. Wainwright, 1861–1865*. New York, 1962.

Nichols, Edward J. *Toward Gettysburg*. State College, Pa., 1969.

Norton, Oliver O. *Army Letters, 1861–1865*. Chicago, 1865.

Osborn, Hartwell. *The Record of the Fifty-fifth Ohio Volunteer Infantry*. Chicago, 1904.

Page, Charles. *The Fourteenth Connecticut*. Meridan, 1906.

Parker, Francis J. *The Story of the Thirty-second Regiment Massachusetts Infantry*. Boston, 1880.

Powell, William. *History of the Fifth Army Corps*. New York, 1886.

Preston, Noble. *History of the Tenth Regiment of Cavalry*. New York, 1892.

Pyne, Henry. *The History of the First New Jersey Cavalry*. Trenton, 1871.

Quaife, Milo M., ed. *From the Cannon's Mouth: The Civil War Letters of General Alpheus S. Williams*. Detroit, 1958.

Roe, Alfred. *The Tenth Regiment Massachusetts Volunteer Infantry*. Springfield, 1909.

Rusling, James. *Men and Things I Saw in the Civil War*. New York, 1889.

Saylor, Daniel P. "The Gospel Visitor." September (1863).

Sedgwick, Henry, ed. *Correspondence of John Sedgwick, Major General 1902*.

Small, Abner. *The Sixteenth Maine Regiment*. Portland, 1886.

Smith, John D. *History of the Nineteenth Regiment Maine Volunteer Infantry*. Minneapolis, 1909.

Sorrel, G. Moxley. *Recollections of a Confederate Staff Officer.* New York, 1917.

Sparks, David S., ed. *Inside Mr. Lincoln's Army: The Diary of General Marsena Patrick, Provost Marshal General, Army of the Potomac.* New York, 1964.

Index

147

orders Sedgwick to Fairfield, 28
dispatches to Henry Halleck, 28, 34, 61
congratulation to the army, 34
orders pursuit, 35–36
letters to his wife, 48, 53, 69, 80, 120
headquarters in Frederick, 62–63
in Middletown, 74
at the Mountain House, 77
at Beaver Creek, 91
Council of War, 95–96, 100
after action report, 127
Middletown, Md., 36, 38, 69, 70, 71, 94, 125,
    129–31
Millerstown, Pa., 24
Monterey Pass, 11, 12, 13, 20, 122
Maritz Crossroads, Pa., 130
Mount Carmel Church, Md., 74, 76
Mount Misery, Md., 71

N

Norton, Oliver, 4, 31, 113

O

Old Frederick Road, 17, 21, 64
Opequon Creek, 107, 122

P

Patrick, Marsena, 3, 25
Pender, Brigadier General Dorsey, 106, 123
Pendleton, Brigadier General William
    Nelson, 120
Petersville, Md., 129–30
Pettigrew, Brigadier General Johnston
    July 3, 1863, viii
    wounded at Falling Waters, 111
    death at Bunker Hill, 111, 120
Pine Stump Road, Pa., 15
Pleasonton, Alfred, 18
Pleasant Valley, Md., 122–23
Powell, William, 4
Purcellville, Va., 129

R

Reynolds, Major General John F.
    loss to Meade, 2
    July 2, 1863, 5
    loss to Katherine Hewitt, 6
    burial in Lancaster, 56, 119
Riddle, Major William, 6
Rodes, Robert, 103
Rohrersville, Md., 129, 131
Rusling, John, 32

S

Saylor, Reverend Samuel, 116
Sedgwick, Major General John
    ordered to Fairfield, 34
    scouting Fairfield, 40–41
    rides south, 65
    Mount Misery, 66, 71
    Funkstown, Md., 86–90
    advance on Williamsport, 115
Sharpsburg, Md., 80, 98, 113
Sickles, Major General Daniel, 32, 96
Sixth U.S. Cavalry, 10
Sixth Virginia Cavalry, 10
Smithsburg, Md., 18, 34, 38
Staunton, Va., 77
Stonebraker, Jacob, 84–87
Strong, George T., 24, 93
Stuart, Major General James E. B., 8, 17,
    19, 97, 98, 107–11, 125
Sykes, George T., 31, 34

T

Taneytown, Md., 13, 36, 129
Taylor, Henry, 31
Thurmont, Md., 130
Turner's Gap, 125, 130
Two Taverns, Pa., 30, 43, 122, 125, 129–30

U

Utica, Md., 31, 36

V

Vicksburg, Miss., 5, 32, 71, 115, 118, 120
Vincent, Colonel Strong, 83

W

Wadsworth General James, 95, 98, 100
Wainwright, Charles, 25, 29, 96, 100
Walkersville, Md., 67, 131
Washington Confederate Cemetery, 88
Waterford, Va., 129
Waterlo, Pa., 85
Waynesboro, Pa., 11, 71
Westminster, Md., 3, 7, 33, 34, 36
Williams, A. S., 122–23
Williamsport, Md., 16, 19, 23, 25, 29, 72, 74,
    86, 91, 93, 96, 104
Wilson, Henry, 92, 112, 113, 126, 130, 131
Winchester, Va., 21, 23
Woodsboro, Md., 22, 36, 70